COGNAC COUNTRY

COGNAC COUNTRY
THE HENNESSY BOOK OF A PEOPLE AND THEIR SPIRIT

Herbert Spencer

PHOTOGRAPHED BY
Fred Mayer

Quiller Press
in association with
Christie's Wine Publications

I
II
III
IV
V
VI

First published 1983 by Quiller Press Ltd
50 Albemarle Street,
London W1X 3HE

Second impression 1984

Copyright © 1983
Illustrations: Société JA^S Hennessy & Co
Text: Herbert Spencer

ISBN 0 907621 23 6

The Endpapers: Old cognac labels from the priceless collection in the
Museum of the Municipality of Cognac.

Designed by Herbert Spencer and Rupert Kirby
Richard Ward (Map)

Produced in consultation with Book Production Consultants,
Cambridge.

Printed in Italy

CONTENTS

APPENDICES

FOREWORD

by Alain de Pracomtal

Président du Directoire, Ja^s Hennessy & Co, Cognac

As a member of one of the oldest cognac families, I have devoted my entire professional life to cognac, and I have never seen a book on the subject which can compare with the present work. In my view, *Cognac Country* is destined to become a classic. It represents a significant and exciting departure from the usual style of books on wines and spirits; its primary appeal is to the senses, as is the unique appeal of a fine cognac.

For many years, the cognac trade has dreamed of a book which would be both informative in words and at the same time portray, through the lens of a master photographer, the region, its people and its product.

When Herbert Spencer and Fred Mayer first asked my advice, I sensed immediately that their approach to the subject could result in such a book, which would enhance the consumer's knowledge and appreciation of cognac.

My advice to them was that the book should not confine itself to one famous cognac house or even several of the larger, well-known firms. It should be a family portrait, using 'family' in its broadest sense, to take in some of the many smaller houses and producers, the thousands of farmers who grow the grapes and make the wine for distilling and the skilled craftsmen who make our stills and the barrels we use for ageing cognac. It should also illustrate something of the history of our region and its life today.

To achieve their goals, Spencer and Mayer have spent much time in our region getting to know us and discovering how we live and work.

Hennessy promised their full support for the book, but as head of the firm I never imagined I would become involved beyond some occasional words of advice. As it turned out, however, I became quite caught up in the work, as did many of my colleagues at Hennessy and in other cognac firms as well.

Over the months, I lost track of the number of times Herbert and Fred appeared outside my office, sometimes unannounced and often dishevelled after a long day's photography in the vineyards. They might have been asking me where to find an old, coal-fired still, or an old press in operation; or telling me about a gem of a Romanesque church they had come across in some remote hamlet, which perhaps I had not seen. They were with us for weeks at a time; in the winter for pruning and grafting, in the spring for the brief flowering of the vines, in the summer for vineyard cultivation, in the autumn for the harvest and wine-making. They photographed coopers and still-makers at work and our tasters creating blends of cognac. They travelled extensively throughout the region observing and photographing other activities. In fact, I can think of no aspect of cognac production, no facet of life in cognac country, which they have not covered in one way or another.

The reader will judge for himself whether the book achieves its goal, but to my mind it is a masterly work and we at Hennessy are proud to have our name associated with it.

Alain de Pracontal

Cognac, 1983

INTRODUCTION

Cognac is renowned throughout the world as the 'king of brandies', the most elegant spirit distilled from wine. It is perhaps less well known that Cognac is also a place whose people and surrounding countryside produce this noble *eau-de-vie*. It is our intention in *Cognac Country* to acquaint the reader with both.

What makes cognac so special? Above all, a combination of land, climate, tradition and dedicated people have given birth to a unique spirit, exclusive to that small corner of France of which Cognac is the centre, which many have tried to imitate but none has matched.

Other grape brandies, including some very drinkable ones, are produced in France and other vine-growing countries. Many types of spirit, notably whisky, gin, vodka and rum, are produced all over the world from varying raw materials and by different means of distillation. Even Scotch, which naturally originated in Scotland, is now often distilled from grain and malt from other countries, and is then sometimes exported in bulk to be blended with whiskies produced elsewhere.

Cognac, however, is produced wholly and solely in two small *départements* in the southwest of France, Charente and Charente-Maritime, in a strictly delimited area no bigger than one of the larger counties of England. Every stage in the making of cognac is exclusively local. The grapes are grown here, the wine is distilled in traditional pot stills manufactured in the region. The barrels for ageing cognac are hand-crafted in local cooperages from wood grown in nearby forests. Even the bottles are produced in a factory in the town of Cognac.

Cognac is created not just by a number of firms whose names appear on the labels, but by many thousands of independent wine growers and distillers who supply the famous cognac houses. The well-known houses and small producers alike are subject to what are probably the most stringent rules and regulations applied to any wines or spirits. Only certain types of grapes may be grown. The wine must be free from additives. Only certain designs and sizes of pot stills are allowed and, unlike some other brandies, cognac must be double-distilled. The cognacs must be of a certain age, depending upon the blend, and names given to blends must be approved by the trade's governing body. Even the labels must have official sanction.

What also sets cognac apart is its price, as every cognac drinker knows. Over the whole range of brands and qualities, cognac is invariably more expensive than other spirits. This is not surprising considering the costly methods used in its production.

We believe that an awareness, born of a close understanding of the land, people and processes involved in the creation of cognac, will enhance the reader's enjoyment and appreciation of this most civilised of spirits.

We have tried to explain in text and captions various terms most frequently used in the production of cognac, and we have provided a glossary for easy reference. However, there are some words and phrases which should be understood from the beginning.

Firstly, the word cognac itself. The official dictionary of French published by the *Académie française*, the guardian of the French language, includes cognac as a generic word, to mean a spirit distilled from white wine produced exclusively in the region centred on the town of Cognac. Since these emminent academicans know the French language better than anyone, we have followed their style in this book: cognac with a small 'c' when referring to the spirit or the region, Cognac with a capital 'C' only when referring to the town itself.

When writing about the making of cognac, we refer many times to the *maître de chais*, a key figure throughout. This title has been translated by others in several ways: literally, it means 'warehouse master,' evoking a foreman in a blue jacket supervising the movement of barrels of ageing cognac, but this is far too modest a term; 'cellar master' is somewhat misleading since cognac is not aged in cellars but above ground; 'chief taster' or 'chief blender' is incomplete in that these functions are only part of his job. In reality, the *maître de chais* of a cognac firm is usually responsible for all aspects of production, from the grape to the glass. He supervises the planting and cultivation of the vineyards, the making and purchasing of wine and its distillation thereafter, the making of barrels for ageing, the ageing and blending of the cognac, and lastly the bottling. It is indicative of the importance of a *maître de chais* that he is usually if not one of the owners of a cognac firm, at least one of its senior directors. So rather than give an inaccurate or incomplete translation of the title, we prefer to retain the original French, *maître de chais*.

In our section on 'The Vine and the Wine,' we have devoted what may seem to be a disproportionate amount of space to the process of grafting vines as a defence against the plague of the root louse *phylloxera* which for the past century has threatened vineyards around the world. In our view, this vital process has been much neglected in other illustrated books on wines and spirits, and we therefore show as much as possible of the grafting process. We are indebted to Jean Peluchon, on whose farm we photographed various stages of grafting throughout the year.

Monsieur Peluchon is only one of the scores of persons who helped us to create this book. When Fred Mayer and I first set out on our travels through cognac country, we were warned that the people of the region were somewhat reserved in character and not inclined to reveal their activities to outsiders. As the weeks and months went by, however, we found the opposite to be true: once they realized we were not simply casual visitors, but were seriously interested in understanding and portraying cognac and the region, all doors were open to us, and we were overcome by cooperation and genuine hospitality.

We were helped by numerous workers and executives of many houses and independent producers, large and small; wine farmers and dairy farmers; local officials; civil and military pilots who flew us over the vineyards; oyster growers who took us out on their boats . . . the list is endless and we could not begin to name all those who gave us their time and assistance. By naming a few we mean to thank them all. This is their book as much as it is ours.

We acknowledge special help from the following:

Pauline Reverchon, curator of Cognac's municipal museum and archives, and author of a small history of the town, who gave us much valuable guidance and allowed us to photograph the museum's priceless collection of old cognac labels.

Jean Taransaud, master cooper of Cognac, author of a learned work on the cooper's art and curator of a unique collection of artifacts now housed in the Hennessy museum; we photographed the craft of barrel-making at the Taransaud cooperage.

Mssrs. Maresté and Prulho, in whose factories we photographed the manufacturing of the traditional copper stills required for the distillation of wine to create cognac.

Gaston Rivière, on whose farm *Domaine des Gatinauds* we photographed what must be the most beautiful old coal-fired stills remaining in the region.

Messrs. Gerald Sturm, Jean-Marie Beulque and others at the governing body of the cognac trade, the *Bureau National Interprofessionnel du Cognac*.

Our most grateful acknowledgements, of course, must go to Hennessy, who gave their wholehearted support to a book which is dedicated to the whole of the cognac trade. We thank all those workers in the Hennessy vineyards, distilleries and warehouses who helped us, as well as Alain de Pracomtal, Gérald de Geoffre, Gilles Hennessy, *maître de chais* Maurice Fillioux, and Hugues Eschasseriaux. They and many others at Hennessy were responsible for making this book a reality.

Herbert Spencer
Cognac, 1983

HISTORY

The enigmatic pile of stones shown on the preceding page is a neolithic dolmen which stands at the edge of a small cognac farmer's vineyard two kilometres east of Kilian Hennessy's Château de St. Brice, north of Cognac. Like Stonehenge in England, it has defied the best efforts of archaeologists to establish exactly why man, thousands of years ago, erected such monuments. Like Stonehenge too, it has stood the ravages of time. This particular dolmen also survived a modern disaster when a jet trainer from the French military base outside Cognac crashed into the vineyard not many metres away.

So the dolmen of Garde-Epée still stands today, with its mantle of lichen, watching over this modern vineyard through the seasons. Was there a vineyard here when neolithic man built it? There are other neolithic remains in the region, including the dolmen of Sèchebec which has been dated at between 2400 and 1800 B.C., indicating there were settlements in and around Cognac at least 4000 years ago. There is another dolmen in a vineyard just outside St.-Fort-sur -le-Ne, south of Cognac, but it is less impressive than the others.

Pauline Reverchon, in her history of Cognac, suggests that the name of the town comes from a Gaulish chieftain, Comnos or Conos, who perhaps held sway in the region before Caesar conquered Gaul. The domain of this chieftain would have become, in Caesar's Latin, *Comniacum* or *Coniacum*. There may have been a Roman *castrum*, or fort, located on the River Charente where Cognac stands today.

A more important Roman centre in the region was at Saintes, between Cognac and the Atlantic coast. One can still see a triumphal arch, built in 19 A.D. and dedicated to the Emperor Tiberius, his son Drusus, and Germanicus, as a votive offering from one Caius Julius Rufius. Roman ruins preserved at Saintes show grape leaves and grapes as carved motifs.

To the south, however, there was Bordeaux, much more important to Imperial Rome, because of its strategic position as an ideal seaport for supplying Rome's conquest and occupation of the British Isles. Bordeaux became a thriving Roman city, one of the most important in Gaul, and Rome helped protect its commercial interests by prohibiting the cultivation of vineyards and the production and export of wine anywhere north of the Gironde River, which included the Charente valley.

It was only towards the end of the 3rd century that the Emperor Probus granted all Gauls the right to produce wine. The valley of the Charente soon became one of the leading wine-producing areas of Roman Gaul, thanks to its temperate climate, its chalky soil, and the river itself which provided easy access to the sea and thence to centres of population elsewhere in France and the Empire. For the next 1000 years and more, the Charente region was to be an important producer and exporter of wines, before cognac was ever thought of.

Like most of Europe, following the fall of the Roman Empire, the Charente region was overrun and suffered at the hands of the Vandals and

Visigoths, Franks, Vikings, and Sarrazins. There is evidence of Frankish occupation of Cognac in the 6th century and of possible Sarrazin occupation before Charles Martel finally turned back the tide of Islam in 732 at Poitiers just to the north. The Vikings who sailed up the Charente in the 9th century to sack Saintes and Angoulême would have passed *Coniacum* and may have enjoyed its wines as well as other pleasures.

The barbarians from the east, north and south were finally driven back or assimilated, but the provinces of Saintonge, Angoumois and Aunis around the Charente were to face centuries more of conflict.

In the 10th century, the first 'lord' of Cognac, Hélie de Villebois, fortified the town and built the first castle worthy of the name, one of a succession of *châteaux* occupying the site on the left banks of the Charente in Cognac.

It was mainly during the 12th century that what remain today the most impressive historical monuments in cognac country, its Romanesque churches, were erected. The pilgrims' road to Santiago de Compostela in northern Spain passed through the Charente valley and gave impetus to the construction of cathedrals, churches and abbeys. Although many of these were destroyed or damaged during the religious wars 300 years later, most still remain and are a major attraction in the area. Guide books list only a few on normal tourist routes, but some of the most charming of the 12th-century churches can be found tucked away in small hamlets among the vineyards.

From the 12th century to the mid 15th century, Cognac was sometimes under English rule, sometimes French. Much of the western half of France as we know it today was ruled by the Plantagenet kings of England until the end of the Hundred Years War in the middle of the 15th century.

Less than a century later the vineyards of the Charentes again became battlefields, this time not political but religious. John Calvin's disciples sought refuge in Angoulême, up river from Cognac, in 1532 and their influence soon spread throughout the region. The bitter religious strife between the followers of Calvin and the Roman Catholics loyal to the French monarchy and the popes ended, at least for a time, with the Edict of Nantes in 1598.

Pauline Reverchon suggests that the Charentais were already distilling some of their wine and exporting *eaux-de-vie* as a single-distillation, unaged and consequently rather rough brandy when the religious wars began in the region. The trade was expanded by the Huguenots, supported by their fellow Protestants in Holland and England, especially after the Edict of Nantes offered greater security to their commercial ventures. Just as the principal towns of the region were Calvinist strongholds – Cognac, Jarnac, Segonzac in the heartland of cognac country, not to mention fortress La Rochelle on the coast – so a large number of the families responsible for developing the cognac trade were Protestant, among them the Delamains and Hines of Jarnac, the Augiers and Martells of Cognac. Many cognac families remained behind during the Huguenot exodus following the Revocation of the Edict of Nantes in 1685; some eventually became Roman Catholic, others are still Protestant.

The cognac trade has always been international – and one could also say ecumenical – in its origins and approach. Wine production and the export of wine started with the Romans and, centuries later, developed under the English and Dutch traders. The Dutch merchants carrying on the wine trade in the region were instrumental in establishing export markets for the *eaux-de-vie* of the Charente.

The most important growth of cognac's international reputation, however, must be credited largely to enterprising families from the British Isles. Many of the best known of the cognac houses today have historic British connections:

The house of Delamain, in Jarnac, was founded by descendants of a local family who emigrated to England and Ireland in the 17th century, gained some prominence there, and returned a century or so later to enter the cognac trade.

Hine, also in Jarnac, was established by a Dorset man, Thomas Hine, who left England in the 18th century to seek his fortune in France.

The house of Martell, one of the two largest today, was founded by a family who moved to Cognac in the 18th century from the British island of Jersey.

The firm of Otard was started by a descendant of an old Scottish family who followed the Stuart King James II into exile after the Stuarts' defeat by William of Orange. Baron Otard bought the Château de Cognac at the end of the 18th century and set up headquarters there.

Hennessy was established in 1765 by the youngest son of the Lord of Ballymacmoy of County Cork, Ireland. Richard Hennessy was a captain in the Irish brigade fighting for the French King Louis XV in the Charente region when he decided to forsake his military career for the cognac trade.

Although extensive production of brandy came relatively late to the cognac region – the Armagnac district was already producing brandy in the 1400s – the *eaux-de-vie* of the Charente valley quickly gained the same reputation for quality, particularly abroad, that the wines of the area had enjoyed for centuries. This was especially true after the practices of double-distillation, ageing in oak barrels and blending took hold.

During the 18th and 19th centuries, when most of the better-known cognac houses were established, cognac farmers and shippers built up substantial stocks of ageing cognac. It was these stocks which carried the cognac region through the crisis of the last two decades of the 19th century, when the plague of the root louse *phylloxera* destroyed virtually all the vineyards in the area and indeed throughout Europe.

It is a matter of pride in the cognac trade that the scientific committees they set up to solve the *phylloxera* problem came up with answers which helped wine farmers around the world to defeat the pest. These local committees established, in 1892, the *Station Viticole de Cognac*, the first research station of its type dealing with viniculture and viticulture and officially supported by the French government. Cognac's research station is still today the most respected in France.

During the years it took to discover the most effective methods of grafting vines to defeat *phylloxera*, to replant lost vineyards and to wait for the new vines to become fully productive, the cognac producers also sought official recognition of their traditional methods of production as well as legal protection of the name of their product. It was in 1900 that French government decrees established the delimited areas of cognac and ruled that the appellation 'cognac' could be applied only to grape brandies produced wholly within the cognac region. Today most countries recognize that, whereas all cognac is brandy, not all brandy is cognac.

The most recent landmark in the history of cognac was the establishment, in 1941, of the Bureau National Interprofessionnel du Cognac. This semipublic body, which includes representatives of all those involved in cognac production – wine farmers, cooperatives, distillers, merchants and shippers – is today a tough-minded watchdog over all aspects of cognac production, distribution and promotion.

Someone once suggested that cognac's international reputation is based largely on astute promotion by the trade over the years and that any area with similar climate and soil could produce just as good a brandy. There may be a grain or two of truth in this, but it raises one very important point: for 400 years, generation after generation, many thousands of Charentais have dedicated themselves to perfecting ideal methods of production and quality control, protected by law when necessary, to create the most elegant spirit in the world. Such dedication, both then and now, has been a major factor in the success and renown of cognac.

This Roman arch beside the River Charente at Saintes, between Cognac and the coast, was built in A.D.19 as a votive offering to Emperor Tiberius, his son, Drusus, and Germanicus.

The Château de Cognac, birthplace of François I, was largely destroyed during the Hundred Years War. The cognac firm Otard preserves remains which include the Hall of Good Count John and the arched Hall of the Guards.

Following pages: Romanesque churches in the village of les Gautiers, surrounded by vineyards, and in Reignac, with flowers on the graves for All Saints Day.

Grotesque carvings on the facade of the Romanesque church in Chateauneuf-sur-Charente contrast sharply in style with the Calvinist austerity of the Protestant *temple* at Segonzac south-east of Cognac. The region was a Huguenot stronghold in the 16th and 17th centuries.

Following pages: the French novelist Pierre Loti called Château de la Roche Courbon 'Sleeping Beauty's Castle'. Dating from the 15th/17th centuries, it is just off the Cognac-Rochefort highway and is open to the public. The 17th-century Château de St. Brice on the banks of the Charente just east of Cognac is owned by M. Kilian Hennessy.

24

Prosperous cognac producers gained prominence in public life in France. Etienne Augier, son of the founder of the oldest existing firm (Augier Freres & Co. 1643), was ennobled by King Louis XVIII in 1815 after serving 26 years as an elected deputy in the National Assembly.

Hennessy's order books, dating from the year the firm was founded by the Irishman Richard Hennessy in 1765, indicate the importance of England as an export market for cognac, yesterday as well as today.

This rare old photograph from Martell's archives shows how cognac was loaded onto sailing barges to be transported down the River Charente to Atlantic ports for export to many countries.

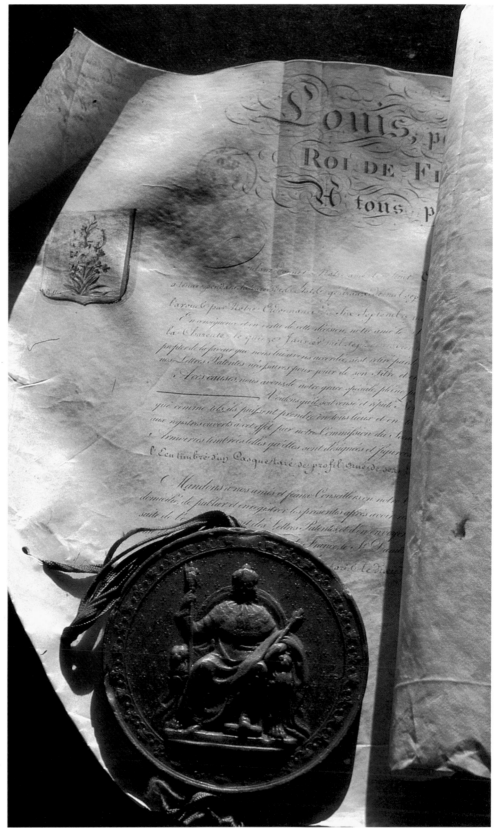

Convince you how much we have your Interest & the
Continuance of your friendship & favours at heart — the
Scribe has impatiently wist for this opportunity of return
you his gratefull thanks for the Civilities you were to
Shew him, we are with the Sincerest Esteem &c

—————————— 2ᵈ Decᵣ 1765 ——————————

Mrˢ Wilkshear West   Mark lane London — as above
- Mr James Tracy.   London   Ditto
- Mrˢ Wᵐ Pitches Thames Street London — Ditto
- Mesⁿ Fonblanque & Tillison   London   Ditto —
- Mr Robᵗ Stevens in the Borrow Southwork London   Dᵒ —
- Mr Jonathⁿ Steell Thames Street   London   Dᵒ —
- Mr Mathⁿ Arbouin 30 Dᵒ   London   Dᵒ
Mr John Ewart Dᵒ Thames Street London —

—————————— 30 Dᵒ ——————————

Mr Thoˢ Mannock London

On the arrival of our Mr B H a few days ago At Charente he
lee the letters you were pleased to fav us with the 19ᵗʰ ulto

31

THE LAND AND THE PEOPLE

France's national highway N10 and more recently the A10 motorway are major routes for tourists seeking the warmth of southern France, Portugal, Spain and North Africa. Year after year millions of French motorists are joined by millions more from the English Channel ferries and from the Low Countries, northern Germany and Scandinavia, most travelling as fast as the heavy traffic will allow in a single-minded dash to the sun, the sea and the beaches. Few pay much heed to the life of provincial France through which they race, and perhaps least of all to that area which lies between the modest cathedral town of Angoulême and the Atlantic coast, halfway along the N10 from Paris to Spain.

Yet the two small provinces between Angoulême and the sea, Charente and Charente-Maritime, are the home of one of France's most famous and prestigious exports, known to all those passing tourists, whatever their nationality: cognac.

Obviously one does not need to visit *les Charentes* to appreciate a glass of cognac, but for the more discerning traveller who wants to learn more about the land, the people and the processes involved in the making of cognac, a leisurely and thoughtful journey through this area is, as the guide books say, well worth a detour. Spend a few days in cognac country and you will learn far more than from technical books on wines and spirits or from travel guides, which often ignore some of the more fascinating aspects of the region.

You could leave the frantic traffic of the N10 at Angoulême or the A10 at Saintes and follow along country roads the River Charente as it meanders gently between Angoulême and the Atlantic coast by way of the town of Cognac itself.

It is easy to lose your way on such roads, even with a good map, but if you do, you might learn by chance something of the essential character of the Charentais, a people dedicated to the creation of cognac. At a country crossroads you flag down a battered 2 CV van to ask directions from the driver, who helps you with patience and understanding and an easy friendliness. But do not be deceived by appearances. This farmer, in muddy boots, old corduroy trousers and well-worn jacket, could well be a 'cognac millionaire'.

His name is unlikely to be Hennessy or Martell or any of the other names you know from the cognac labels, but his family may have been making cognac for just as long as they have. If you are lucky enough to be invited to his home for a glass or two of his private reserve, he may seat you at a kitchen table with a plastic tablecloth and never mention that he has millions of francs worth of cognac ageing in old oak barrels in the barn next door. He may entertain you in his shirt-sleeves and you would never guess that, out of sight in his somewhat ramshackle farm buildings, he has modern tractors, vineyard cultivators, perhaps even a mechanical grape-picking machine; the latest model grape press and fermenting tanks for making wine; a gleaming new, gas-fired copper pot still replacing the coal-fired veteran finally retired after serving his family for generations; a small fleet of cars, perhaps even a

Mercedes, for use by the numerous members of his hard-working family.

This independent Charentais farmer and distiller of cognac will never boast to you about his acres of vineyards or his modern equipment. He, in common with hundreds of other independent cognac producers – and the term 'cognac millionaire' is not necessarily an exaggeration in certain cases – is most discreet about his wealth and most careful about what he does with it. He usually uses it to buy more land to plant more vineyards to produce more wine which he can distill into more *eau-de-vie* which he ages in his barns until the right moment arrives to sell it to the big cognac firms. His family has been doing this for generations; their wealth is in the land and the vines and the cognac, all of which they can pass on to their heirs along with their expertise and dedication to cognac. The Charentais character is, in this respect, a guarantee of the unique and enduring character of cognac itself.

As you travel through the region, you will soon discover that its prosperity does not come solely from cognac, although cognac is the greatest source of its wealth and international reputation. This region is rich in agriculture: fields of abundant wheat and corn and other crops are generally just as much in evidence as vineyards. Extensive pastures, including the water meadows created by the annual flooding of the Charente, support a dairy industry which is known principally for its butter, more valued by many French chefs and gastronomes than the butter of Normandy. The coastal area produces the famous oysters of Marennes and other shellfish renowned through France and beyond.

Throughout the Charentes, however, the character of the Charentais remains essentially the same, a friendly but serious people who eschew any ostentatious display of their success. The grand châteaux, unlike those of the Loire and other areas, are often unoccupied relics of the past, but around every corner there is a substantial working farm, many almost like manors but prudently hiding their prosperity behind high, old walls and weathered wooden doors.

You see many such farms as you make your way into the heartland of the region, to Cognac, the titular capital and the focal point of your exploration of cognac country.

To the casual traveller passing through its centre, Cognac appears not very different from any other French provincial town of 25,000 or so inhabitants. In the main square a few cafés, a modest hotel, and a local branch of the ubiquitous modern department store encircle an equestrian statue of Francis I, King of France, who was born here in 1494. At harvest time gendarmes pluck itinerant grape pickers from the well tended flower beds around the statue, firmly encouraging them to congregate elsewhere. There is a large municipal market a few streets away and during the day the centre is busy and the traffic around *Place François I* can be exasperating. After eight at night, however, the streets are nearly deserted thanks to the self-imposed social curfew of the provincial French who believe that respectability means spending the evening in one's own home with the family. If there is a major soccer or rugby match on television, the curfew falls even earlier.

It is only when you wander away from the centre, down towards the river, that you begin to realise that there is something very special about this small town of Cognac.

In the old quarter between the municipal market and the River Charente, you find narrow, cobblestoned streets lined with shuttered houses, some dating back to medieval times. Their ancient stones and tiled roofs are covered with a strange patina as black, and sometimes as heavy, as the accumulation of soot inside an unswept chimney. These houses are not victims of modern pollution, but are proudly wearing a living mantle, a black fungus that thrives upon the fumes from the many thousands of barrels of ageing cognac. The evaporation of cognac from the warehouses is romantically termed 'the angels' share', a very generous portion indeed considering that, in volume, it equals the total amount of cognac consumed in France in a year. You see such blackened walls and roofs wherever cognac is ageing, in the towns and villages and on the farms.

The cobblestones of old Cognac, sometimes glistening from the frequent rains which succour the vineyards, lead you down to a broad quay on the banks of the Charente. Here, for almost three centuries, cognac was loaded on to barges for transport down river to the seaports and thence by ship to the world. Sadly the last remaining examples of Charente cognac barges were destroyed during the Second World War; had they survived, they would be treasured museum pieces. The clatter of horse-drawn drays on the cobblestones as they brought barrels down to the barges is only an echo in the memories of a few, long-retired warehouse workers.

The cobblestones of the quay have been paved over and heavy road transport has replaced the barges, but the banks of the Charente remain as busy as ever. The two largest cognac firms, Hennessy and Martell, and some smaller ones, including Otard in the ancient Château de Cognac, still maintain their headquarters on or just by the quay. It is from them or from other firms in Cognac or the other principal towns of the region that you can learn most about cognac. Most of the big firms, and many of the smaller ones, welcome visitors (see Appendices) and proudly show them around their premises. There are also occasional tours, according to the season, of vineyards and distilleries in the countryside.

After instructive visits to the cognac houses, and perhaps a tasting, you may find it a welcome break to follow the Charente down to the sea by way of Saintes with its Roman ruins and to visit La Rochelle, just north of the mouth of the river. The old port of La Rochelle, which was once the main point of departure for cognac exports abroad, still retains a charming air of antiquity and offers excellent seafood in restaurants along the quay. La Rochelle is an important yachting centre as well as a busy fishing port.

To the south of La Rochelle, beyond the mouth of the Charente, lies the sprawling estuary of the river Seudre and kilometre after kilometre of oyster parks and oyster beds which extend far out into the shallows between

Marennes, centre of the oyster industry, and the island of Oléron. You may find a friendly skipper who will lend you a pair of hip boots and take you out to sea with him at low tide to watch the cultivation and gathering of the oysters on the exposed banks. The departure and return of the oyster fleet, an armada of hundreds of boats, are impressive sights from the bridge across the estuary or from the viaduct connecting Oléron with the mainland. The most spectacular view of the oyster parks is from the air; it is easy to find a light plane to take you up from the small airfield at Marennes or from the Aero Club at nearby Royan-Médis airport.

Back in the heartland of the cognac region, an aerial view of the vineyards around Cognac, Jarnac and Segonzac is also well worth the small fee for the hire of a plane and pilot. There is an Aero Club just outside Cognac sharing runways with a military base which is the centre for basic jet training of French Air Force and Navy pilots.

But perhaps the best way to get to know cognac country is simply to drive around as the whim takes you. Whatever the time of year there are landscapes of spectacular beauty.

Take your time. The Charentais are sometimes called *cagouillards*, from the local name for edible snails which form the basis of one of their regional dishes. The snail is slow but sure, which is the way cognac is made and also the best way for you to get to know this land and its people.

Previous pages: the river on the outskirts of Cognac provides a quiet Sunday's fishing.
Training jets from the air base just outside Cognac fly in formation over the vineyards.

Birds feeding on grapes become prey themselves in the vineyards of cognac. A mushroom-hunting foray provides a rare sighting of the virtually extinct bonnet called *quichenotte*, from English 'kiss me not!'

Shifting barrels of cognac provides muscle-building for players on local teams in a region where rugby is an immensely popular sport. Less muscle, but as much skill is needed for *boules* in a Cognac square.

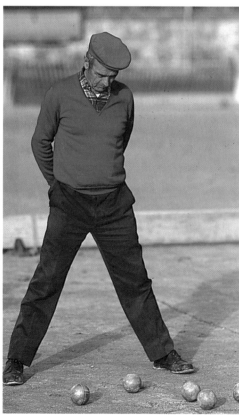

René Firino-Martell, head of Martell, chats with Alain de Pracomtal, president of Hennessy, after the wedding of his daughter in Cognac's main church. Strong rivalry among cognac houses leaves room for personal friendship outside the office.

The central square of the town of Cognac, dominated by an equestrian statue of King François I who was born here and who met King Henry VIII on the field of 'The Cloth of Gold'.

From the air, one can see along the quay Otard's Château de Cognac; the medieval city gate; the headquarters of Hennessy and, above right, Martell's warehouses. Hennessy use boats to ferry visitors over to their warehouses on the opposite bank among the trees.

A black fungus thriving on the alcohol evaporating from thousands of barrels of ageing cognac in the town's warehouses gives a patina to the roofs and walls of old Cognac.

Following pages: A spring boat race on the Charente in front of Hennessy.

Other important towns in the region include Jarnac, upriver from Cognac, where Courvoisier, Delamain, Hine and other firms have their headquarters.

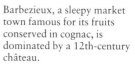

Barbezieux, a sleepy market town famous for its fruits conserved in cognac, is dominated by a 12th-century château.

The historic Atlantic port of La Rochelle, with its three towers of St. Nicholas, the Chain and the Lantern, is still an active fishing town as well as a famous yachting centre.

Following pages: south of La Rochelle, the estuary of the River Seudre is filled with hundreds of square kilometres of man-made *parcs* where oysters fatten in shallow ponds.

49

The cultivation of oysters is an intensive commercial activity in the region. Oysters are planted out and develop in prepared beds in the tidal waters of the Marennes-Oléron Basin, to be harvested at low tide throughout the year.

An armada of hundreds of small boats bring the crop to ports on the island of Oléron, seen here, and at Marennes and La Tremblade in the Seudre estuary.

In the *parcs*, the oysters grow fat on the algae called *navicule* which gives them their green colour as well as their delicate taste. It is two years or more before the largest of the oysters of Marennes find their way onto platters throughout France and abroad.

Dairy farming is another major source of wealth in the region. The annual flooding of the Charente provides rich pasturing for the spring and summer and large fields amongst the vineyards produce abundant fodder for the winter.

The small town of Mirambeau, close to the southern frontier of cognac country, is important for its cattle market. Hundreds of head are bought and sold during the year, to renew dairy herds.

This boy is herding cows home for evening milking. Much of the milk goes into production of excellent butter. The butter of the Charentes is considered by some to be superior to the best from Normandy.

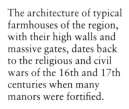

The architecture of typical farmhouses of the region, with their high walls and massive gates, dates back to the religious and civil wars of the 16th and 17th centuries when many manors were fortified.

Roofs covered with black fungus shows where cognac is stored on the farms.

Cognac is volatile, so every hamlet has its fire precautions. In Cognac, Hennessy and Martell have their own fire brigades to support the municipal units in protecting the millions of barrels of cognac ageing in the town.

Staves of oak are stacked in the open, to weather for several years before they are fashioned into the barrels necessary to the ageing of cognac.

The inhabitants of cognac have been said to be somewhat slow, earning themselves the nickname *cagouillards* after the fat snails which feed in the vineyards and which form the base of one of the regional dishes.

A dairy farmer and a cattle salesman at the livestock market in Mirambeau.

A competitor in a regional brass band contest by the keep of an ancient château, traditional seat of Lords of Pons whose power gave rise to the adage 'If you can't be the King of France, you would want to be the Lord of Pons'.

One of cognac country's 37,000 wine growers and his son in their barn at harvest time.

Jacques de Varenne, head of the oldest cognac firm, in his office and tasting room just off the quay in Cognac.

VINE AND WINE

Since the days of Roman occupation, the ancient provinces of Saintonge, Angoumois and Aunis have together constituted one of the most important wine-producing areas of France. The wines from in and around the Charente Valley were known and appreciated in England, the Low Countries and Scandanavia. Today the same region produces more white wine than any comparable area in the world, yet little of the wine of Charente is sold in the bottle and certainly none of any quality or international reputation.

This apparent paradox is easily explained. The vast quantity of wine now produced in the region is not for drinking but for distilling to make cognac.

Many of the thousands of wine farmers of the cognac region reserve small quantities of grapes from their vineyards to make wine for their own use. There is still a small commercial production of wine, both red and white, for largely local consumption. Most Charentais, however, drink *vin ordinaire* from the supermarkets, or wines of quality from the neighbouring Bordeaux region or other areas of France.

The white wine produced by the Charentais in millions of hectolitres each year is probably the purest, most natural wine one could imagine. Stringent regulations control its production, forbidding the use of additives, for these would taint the wine and ruin the finished cognac. Thin and acid, with no pretensions to ageing, it is not a wine one would choose to drink. It is, however, the perfect wine for distillation.

Not all the wines of Charente are the same. During the 18th and 19th centuries cognac farmers and shippers recognized that different areas of the Charente region supported vineyards that produced wines of different character, which in turn, when distilled, resulted in *eau-de-vie* of varying qualities, some more desirable than others for ageing cognac. These traditional sub-regions were already well defined before the French government decree of May 1, 1909 which established the delimited region of cognac production giving them legal and geographical form.

The names of the six officially designated growth areas or *crus* reflect the general nature of the regions as they were in past centuries. The word '*champagne*', as in the *crus* of Grande Champagne and Petite Champagne, indicates that this was open country, meadows or moorlands; '*borderies*' indicates an adjoining area; '*bois*', as in the *crus* of Fins Bois, Bons Bois and Bois Ordinaires or Bois Communs, indicates that these areas were once heavily wooded, although that is less true today.

The four most important sub-growths are Grande Champagne, Petite Champagne, Borderies, and Fins Bois, all of which contribute to the finest blends of cognac according to the character of the *eau-de-vie* originating in their vineyards.

La Grande Champagne is the most heavily cultivated by cognac farmers with 40% of its 35,700 hectares under vine. It encompasses 27 *communes*, or parishes, extending to the southeast of the town of Cognac, with the River Charente from west of Cognac to east of Jarnac as its northern boundary. At its centre is the small town of Segonzac, which proclaims itself 'the Capital of Grande Champagne'.

The 'capital' Segonzac is actually more a village than a town. It has an unpretentious church on the square, a Protestant *temple*, the usual complement of village shops and cafés and one modest restaurant whose reputation extends beyond the local clientele.

Drive in any direction out of Segonzac, however, and you will find extensive vineyards covering the rolling hills and numerous farms, large and small, with their own distilleries and black-roofed warehouses containing thousands of barrels of ageing cognac. This is the rich heart of cognac country.

The Grande Champagne is favoured by its chalky soil, which built up during the Cretaceous period. The sub-soil is chalky clay; the top soil includes more friable chalk. Its situation mid-way between the sea and the higher ground to the east of the Charente Valley creates a very temperate microclimate. Soil and climate combine to provide ideal conditions for growing the white grapes and making the wine for distillation into *eau-de-vie de cognac*.

La Petite Champagne cradles the *crus* of Grand Champagne in a crescent to the south, east and west with a tiny enclave north of the river around Bourg-Charente between Cognac and Jarnac. It comprises 60 *communes* and 25% of its 68,400 hectares are under vine.

This sub-region includes the small towns of Chateauneuf-sur-Charente and Archiac and the larger towns of Jonzac and Barbezieux, the latter known not only for its production of chestnuts and various fruits preserved in cognac, but also for the only restaurant in the region rating a star in the Guide Michelin.

There is little difference between Grande Champagne and Petite Champagne as regards climate and soil and the grapes and wine they produce. The micro-climate is virtually the same. The top soil of Petite Champagne is generally as rich in calcium, but more compacted. Some vineyards, especially around Archiac, are said to equal many of the Grande Champagne in the quality of the *eau-de-vie* they produce.

Les Borderies is by far the smallest of the sub-regions, but one of the most favoured with 30% of its 13,440 hectares under vine. It consists of only six *communes* located between the town of Cognac and the village of Burie to the northwest. Its soil contains perhaps half the calcium of that of the Grande Champagne, but is very rich and grows very fine grapes, whose wine boasts the flavour and aroma of violets. Its *eau-de-vie* is therefore much in demand, but it produces only about 5% of that used in ageing cognac. Historically the wines of the Borderies were highly prized, and today the village of Burie is the self-styled 'Capital of Pineau', the aperitif made with grape juice and cognac aged together.

Les Fins Bois forms a broad belt around the first three *crus* and includes 278 *communes*, most to the north and east of Cognac with a small southern enclave outside the belt between the market town of Mirambeau and the estuary of the Gironde. Only about 10% of its 345,000 hectares are under vine, but because of its size it produces almost 40% of the *eau-de-vie* for cognac.

Angoulême, the administrative capital of the Departement of the Charente, and Saintes, a major town of the Charente-Maritime, both lie within this large sub-region, as do the historic towns of Pons and St. Jean d'Angély, an important wine-growing centre when the wines of the Charente were being exported in quantity. Throughout most of this *cru*, however, grain crops and dairy farming are much more in evidence than vineyards.

The sub-soil of the Fins Bois is composed of compacted chalk, but the top soil is much less rich in calcium. Geographically the area is still central enough not to be unduly influenced by climatic conditions from the sea and the interior, although because of its size it is more subject to local variations than the first three *crus*.

Les Bon Bois encircles the first of four *crus* in a belt that is much more exposed to climatic influences from the sea to the west, and from the higher land beyond the Charente basin to the east. Its soil is much poorer in calcium than that of the first four *crus*. *Les Bois Ordinaires*, also sometimes referred to as *Les Bois Communs*, is the last sub-region that lies along the Atlantic coast and includes two islands, Ile D'Oléron and Ile de Ré, and a very small enclave to the far southeast of the delimited area of cognac. Less than 4% of the 660,776 hectares of these two *crus* are under vine. The Bons Bois produces just over 20% of the *eaux-de-vie* for cognac, even though some firms turn their backs on it. The Bois Ordinaires vineyards produce almost as much red wine for drinking as white wine for distilling. This coastal sub-region is much better known for, and makes a great deal more money from, its shellfish, fishing and tourist industries than its *eaux-de-vie*.

Less than 10% of the whole cognac region is devoted to vineyards and, unlike some other wine-producing areas, there are few large holdings, This is a region of small wine farmers: some 35,000 farmers work less than 100,000 hectares under vine, so the average size of a congac vineyard is slightly less than 3 hectares.

Every grower, large or small, must conform strictly to the regulations laid down by the cognac Bureau with regard to the growing of grapes and making of wine for cognac distillation. The wine for distilling *eaux-de-vie de cognac* must come from specified grape varieties, and only three are approved for general use: Ugni Blanc, known locally as St. Emilion des Charentes, accounts for more than 90% of the vines; Folle Blanche and Colombard, once popular, are today out of favour and rarely grown. Several secondary varieties are permitted, but only up to a maximum of 10% in the vineyards of the region. The total number of hectares under vine in each of the six *crus* is controlled, with new plantings requiring approval, but the total crop is not restricted, which is one reason why the higher yield of the St. Emilion des Charentes makes it the most popular variety.

Generally vineyard cultivation in cognac is the same as elsewhere, save for one or two important restrictions. Except for newly planted vines, irrigation is forbidden and the grapes are picked somewhat before they reach full maturity to keep down the sugar content and ensure acidity.

During the winter vines are carefully pruned by hand and trained along wires. For new plantings and replacements vines that were grafted the previous year and grown through the summer in open nurseries are planted out in the winter months. The vines flower in June or early July, and undergo a secondary pruning, by machines in the larger vineyards, to remove excess foliage and concentrate growth in the new-born grapes.

The harvest usually begins in October and goes on through much of November, depending upon the weather and the micro-climates of the various vineyards. Because of the vast amount of fruit to be picked and rising labour costs, the region is increasingly turning to mechanical grape-picking machines, as are many other wine-producing areas in the world. Some larger wine producers have their own machines, others are maintained by cooperatives. Much of the crop, however, is still brought in by hand by cognac farmers and their families joined by itinerant contract pickers.

There are few of the old style vertical wine presses remaining in the region. Most pressing today takes place in modern, horizontal presses. The use of the Archimedes, or continuous press is prohibited, for it would crush the stems and skins and release substances that would affect the distilled spirit. For the same reason the addition of sulphur, common in most wine-making, is forbidden. Also forbidden is the addition of sugar to the must, a frequent practice elsewhere, to increase the alcohol content of the wine. Again, the object in cognac is to produce a thin, somewhat acidic wine of low alcohol content, free of all additives which could influence the finished product.

The pure grape must, or juice, goes into large concrete tanks where fermentation takes place in one to two weeks by the action of the natural yeasts on the grape. The tanks are then sealed to preserve the wine until it goes to the stills.

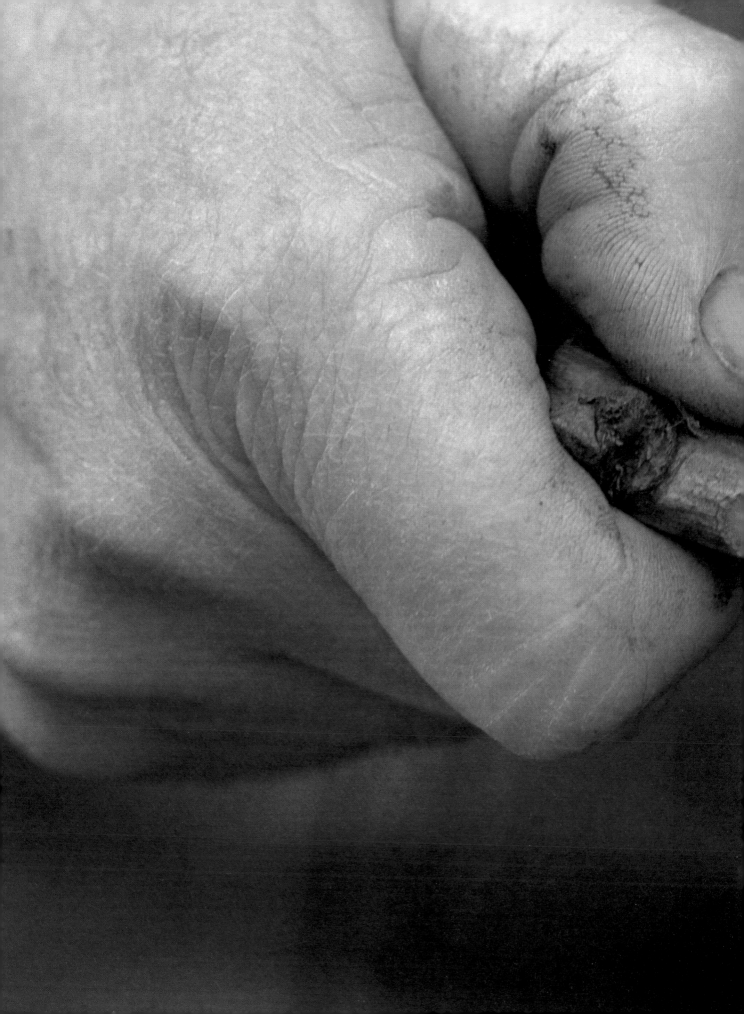

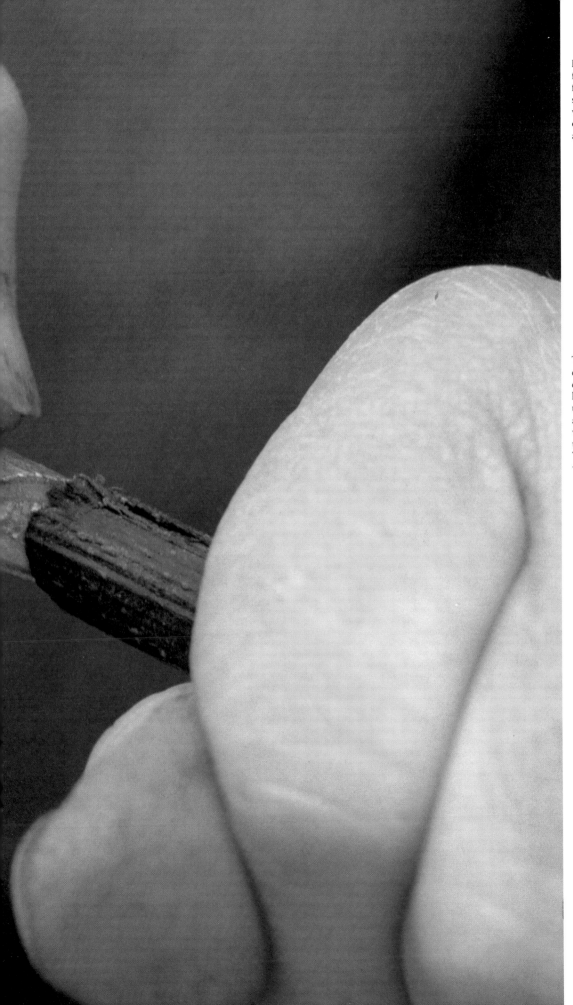

Previous pages: some cognac farmers produce vine grafts, for their own use and for sale to others, to renew vineyards or establish new ones. Grafting takes place at the end of winter.

The grafts are created by carefully joining a small cutting from one of the locally approved varieties, usually Ugni Blanc, with a cutting from American vines which are resistant to the root louse *Phylloxera*. The local cutting, left, will bear the fruit.

Grafts are dipped in wax to protect the delicate joins, then stored in boxes under blankets of humus and left to consummate the marriage of the two types of vines.

Within two months or so, grafts have taken, showing tender young leaves on the fruit stock and rudimentary root structure, and are ready for planting in nurseries.

The grafted vines grow at a great rate during the summer. They are taken up and stored over the winter and are ready for their permanent homes the next spring.

This one nursery field, less than 100 metres a side, has more than 120,000 new grafts growing in rich soil covered with sheets of black plastic to retain heat and moisture.

In late winter, when sap is at its lowest, the vines are pruned by hand. Some of the prunings are burned in the vineyards, some are cut up as mulch to enrich the soil and some are kept for burning at home, giving a unique flavour to foods cooked over the grill.

Once pruned, the branches which will bear fruit are bent and tied by hand, in a traditional, prescribed manner. Usually the men in the family do the harder work of pruning, the women take on the less strenuous but equally demanding task of shaping the vines.

74

During the growing season, from spring through to the autumn harvest, the vines require constant attention, including spraying several times to protect them from pests and mildew, pruning leaves to concentrate growth in the bunches of grapes and weeding.

Much of the work is done by specially designed and carefully adjusted machines, but weeding between the individual vines must still be done by hand.

These two views of the
same vineyards, in winter
and then in the early
autumn when the grapes
are ready for harvesting,
typify the changing
landscapes of the region
throughout the year.

Usually none but the farmer
in his vineyard notes the
very brief flowering of the
vines which occurs in late
spring, the moment when
the grapes are born, in
bunches which will be
ready for picking in about
three months' time.

77

In the Charentes, grapes are picked early, before they have reached their full maturity, in order to ensure a lower sugar content to make the low-alcohol wine preferred for distillation into *eau-de-vie de cognac*.

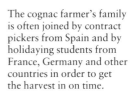

The cognac farmer's family is often joined by contract pickers from Spain and by holidaying students from France, Germany and other countries in order to get the harvest in on time.

Because of the vast amount of fruit which must be harvested at just the right stage of maturity, the cognac region is making increasing use of grape-picking machines, owned by larger growers or shared by a number of smaller vineyards. One machine manned by three workers can do the job of large numbers of men and women picking by hand.

Machines must be carefully adjusted to straddle rows of vines as they move slowly through the vineyard shaking off the grapes. Mechanical pickers do not harm the vines, nor is the quality of the wine affected.

82

Picking grapes is hard work, in the hot sun or pouring rain. At day's end, pickers head back to the farmhouses for very substantial meals provided by the vineyard proprietors.

One young helper in a small, private vineyard near Cognac gets a welcome ride home from a friend.

Following page: there are few old-type presses still working in cognac country, with even small wine farmers installing modern units. This old press was at Eric Hennessy's estate La Gibauderie, near Jarnac.

83

The old presses require more manpower, but still do the job efficiently. New or old, the presses are designed to avoid crushing stems, which might affect the flavour of cognac.

The skins and stems left from the pressings are used as a natural fertilizer to enrich the soil of the vineyards.

One of the most modern units for wine-making is at Bisquit, near Rouillac northeast of Cognac, with six large presses in a row. The grape juice, the must, is piped directly into large fermentation tanks.

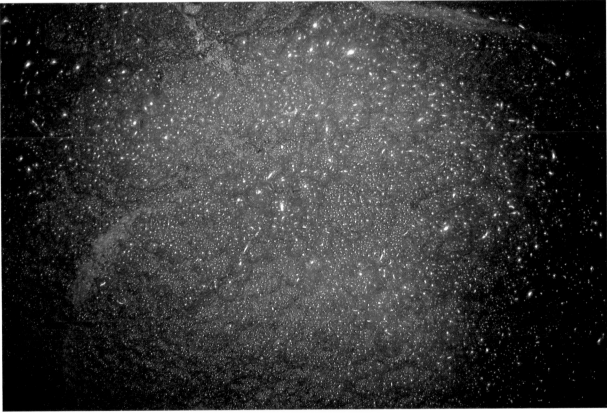

DISTILLING THE SPIRIT

The alchemists of the Middle Ages made much use of the process of distillation in their futile search for methods of transforming base metals into precious metals. The alchemists never succeeded in turning lead into gold or iron into silver, but by perfecting the still to serve their flights of fancy, they did contribute to the eventual creation of the golden liquid we know today as cognac.

The process of distillation is one of the most basic physical reactions, as old as the earth itself and one of the first principles of physics we learn in school. Water on the earth's surface is heated by the sun until it becomes a vapour, which rises into the atmosphere, free of all impurities whether salt from the sea or minerals from the land. Once cooled in the atmosphere, the water vapour condenses into liquid and falls back to earth as rain.

Our words 'distil', 'distillation', 'still', etc. come from the Latin *stillare* (to drop) and *di* (one by one), but the process was known to man long before the Romans practised it. The Egyptians extracted essences from herbs and flowers by distillation; the Chinese may have made a rice spirit; the Greeks made turpentine from resin.

It was left to the followers of the prophet Mohammed, despite his prohibition against the consumption of fermented wine or spirits, to introduce into western Europe during the Middle Ages the idea of distilling wine into spirits. Even the words 'alcohol' and 'alambic', the term still used by the French for a still, are from the Arabic.

The alchemist's still was the primitive ancestor of the pot still, which is still in use today. In its simplest form it was a boiler into which a liquid was placed and heated until parts of it became vapour. The vapour rose into a collecting chamber at the top of the boiler. Originally the vapour simply passed through a pipe exposed to the cold air where it condensed as it cooled and trickled out as a purified liquid. Stills were later refined and made somewhat more efficient by extending the pipe from the collecting chamber through a bath of cold water, thereby speeding up the condensation.

Adaptation of the basic still to turn wine into a more or less pure alcohol spirit was the next step. Water boils and turns into vapour at 100° Centigrade (212° Fahrenheit), but alcohol vapourizes at the lower temperature of 78.3°C (173°F). Therefore when wine is heated in the still, its alcohol content passes out first, leaving the water behind. Whatever other elements in the wine were left behind with the water or retained in the spirit eventually became part of the art of the distiller.

In the early 19th century efforts were made to improve upon the efficiency of distillation, as the pot still is a relatively slow and inefficient method of extracting spirit from wine or other materials. The design most used today for making whisky, gin, vodka and many grape brandies other than cognac was invented by an Irishman, Aeneas Coffey, and is variously referred to as the Coffey, column or continuous still.

The cognac region, however, has stuck by the traditional pot still that has been in use for centuries. Although slow, it allows for a more delicate control of the distillation, and by rectifying the spirit to a lesser degree also leaves in the cognac more of the original flavour and aroma of the wine, providing a spirit of more marked character.

The reputation of the skilled craftsmen who make cognac stills extends far beyond the borders of cognac country. If you visit one of their factories, you may see workmen fashioning parts that are much too small for use here. They are making small stills used in the production of rice spirits for clients in southeast Asia.

The atmosphere in a cognac stills factory has a dramatic, almost theatrical quality. The noise is deafening but with a certain cadence. Great shapes of gleaming copper fill the vast halls. Flames from large blow torches play on sheets of copper heating it into patches of iridescent colours. A black-bearded man, muscles bulging, strikes at the copper with a great wooden mallet. Another worker hammers away at a smaller piece already coloured blood-red with a thick coating of protective wax. The worker who applied the wax by hand adds a comic touch when he declares, 'It takes me two weeks to get this colour of blood off my hands and my wife won't let me touch her until I have.' His small sacrifice ensures that the exterior of the still on which he was working will be protected for up to 50 years by its wax coating.

The traditional Charentais pot still made entirely of copper. Although expensive this is the metal least likely to be attacked by the acid in the wine, as well as retaining some of the more unpleasant by-products of distillation, thereby purifying the spirit.

In the basic Charentais still a boiler (*chaudière*) is bricked in with a heat source. Originally wood was used as fuel for the furnace, then coal, but today most stills use natural gas. Electricity is not permitted, since, by law, the cognac still must be heated by an open flame. Atop the boiler, above the brick work, is the still head (*chapiteau*), either onion or turban shaped, which can be removed to allow the boiler to be cleaned after each distillation. The alcohol vapours collect in the still head which is surmounted by a gracefully shaped pipe, the swan's neck (*col de cygne*). The alcohol vapours pass to the condenser through this pipe. The condenser consists of a coil of copper pipe (*serpentin*) immersed in a large tank of continuously flowing cold water. The cold water cools the vapour until it becomes liquid alcohol which trickles slowly out into a waiting barrel.

Some cognac stills also include a chamber for pre-heating the wine to be distilled (*chauffe-vin*). The pipe carrying the hot vapours from the still head to the condenser passes through this tank, raising the temperature of the wine and lowering the temperature of the vapours. Whereas the basic design of the cognac still is regulated by law, the use of the wine pre-heater is optional. Although it increases the efficiency of the still to a degree, it is a costly piece of equipment to install and maintain.

The capacity of cognac stills is also regulated by law. For the second distillation the maximum capacity is 25 hectolitres. For the first distillation larger stills, usually 50 or 100 hectolitres, may be used, but many small growers employ the older, 12½ hectolitre size, and even some 3 hectolitre stills continue to operate.

In the cognac region distillation begins soon after the first wine has fermented. By law, distillation could begin as early as September, but in practice the larger distillers do not begin much before the first week of November when sufficient quantities of wine have fermented to keep the stills busy 24 hours a day. The start of distillation naturally depends on whether the grape harvest is early or late in that particular year. Some small farmers, who may take longer to bring in the harvest, sometimes do not start distilling until early in December.

The law requires that all distilling of wine produced in the autumn must be finished by May 31. In practice, however, many distillers finish work a month or so earlier. This means that the more productive stills will have been at work day and night for close on six months of the year, allowing some time off for holidays. The process of distilling *eau-de-vie de cognac* is a slow one.

Of the more than 35,000 wine farmers in the cognac region, some 5,000 are also distillers. There are two categories of distillers: the *bouilleurs de cru*, who distill only their own wines, and the *bouilleurs de profession*, who distill not only their own wine (if indeed they produce any), but also wine from other farmers. The number varies from year to year, but there are normally about 3,000 stills operating in the region, some shared by several independent distillers.

Even the most modest wine farmer in the region has the right to distil *eau-de-vie* for cognac, so long as he abides by the regulations laid down by the Bureau. His distillery may consist of only one or perhaps two very old 12½ hectolitre stills in the corner of one of his barns. He may still use coal to fuel the furnace and, working on his own, he may have a camp bed beside his still in order to catch a few hours sleep at night. A cognac still is a very demanding mistress: the farmer will be awakened more than once during the night by his alarm clock reminding him to stoke the fire or check the *eau-de-vie* trickling from his still into an old barrel.

At the other end of the scale is Bisquit's Lignères distillery near Rouillac northeast of Cognac, with 56 stills operating in one vast hall. The Bisquit distillery, by far the largest in the region, is highly automated and much of the distillation process is controlled by one man at a large console in a glass booth overlooking the hall.

Much more typical of the modern distilleries operated by the large cognac houses which do part of their own distilling is that of Hennessy at Le Peu, near the village of Juillac-le-Coq in the centre of the Grande Champagne district. Le Peu has ten 25-hectolitre, gas-fired stills in its central hall. The distillery, with its red-tiled floor and spotless stills, is considered a showplace by Hennessy, who sometimes use it for prestige lunches or dinners for up to 300 guests. During the distillation season the strong aroma of fumes from the stills adds a special touch to these functions.

Ideally the wine to be distilled for *eau-de-vie de cognac* should be between 7° and 8° in alcohol strength. Its acidity has helped preserve it from the time of its fermentation to its arrival at the still. It is neither racked nor filtered, since its lees contributes to the character of the *eau-de-vie*. It takes about nine litres of this low-strength wine to make one litre of *eau-de-vie de cognac* after the process of double-distillation.

The first distillation of the wine (*première chauffe*) takes about eight hours and results in a rather unpleasant-tasting milky liquid with an alcoholic strength of around 28° (*brouillis*). The distiller must control the *première chauffe* throughout to ensure that the wine has been properly reduced in the boiling, vapourizing and condensation.

It is in the second distillation (*bonne chauffe*) that the distiller must exercise all his skills and experience with the greatest of care. The character and quality of the *eau-de-vie* from this final distillation will determine to a great extent the character and quality of cognac after ageing.

After the stills have been cleaned, as they must be between each distillation, the *brouillis* from the *première chauffe* is pumped back into the stills. It takes the *brouillis* from three first distillations to charge the still for the second, and the second goes more slowly, taking up to 12 hours.

The most delicate part of the whole distillation process is the separation of the 'head' (*tête*) and 'tail' (*queue*) from the 'heart' (*coeur*). The first and last parts of the distillation carry substances which would add unwanted flavours and smells to the cognac but also contain precious alcohol and minute quantities of the elusive elements which characterize the taste and bouquet of cognac. They are therefore set aside for further treatment in a later *chauffe*.

The distiller, therefore, takes only the heart of the *bonne chauffe* to make cognac. This *eau-de-vie de cognac* trickles out of the still as a colourless liquid of an average strength of 70° alcohol, close to twice the strength of the spirits we normally drink.

To taste this fresh *eau-de-vie* can best be described as an experience rather than a pleasure; it is fiery to the tongue and throat and, for the layman, has little flavour and only a slight aroma of fruit or flowers.

The experienced distiller, however, and especially the *maître de chais* can sense from this first tasting what kind of cognac a particular *eau-de-vie* will become after years of ageing in oak barrels and blending with those of other vineyards and vintages.

Preceding pages: at the
Maresté factory in Cognac,
sheets of bright copper are
heated and hammered into
shape in heavy steel moulds.

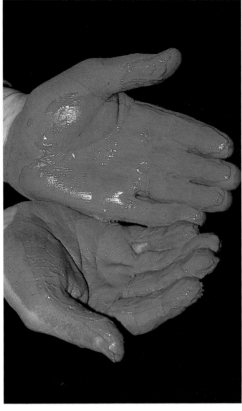

The outsides of the stills
are coated with a heavy wax
mixture sometimes referred
to as 'mayonnaise'. Smaller
parts are still coated by
hand; larger parts are
coated by machine.

The wax is hammered into
the copper by machine or
by hand, with hammers which
must be highly polished.

At the Prulho factory just
outside Cognac, the parts
of a traditional still are
assembled with copper rivets.

This old still illustrates
the basic design of a cognac
pot still which has changed
little in 400 years:

On the right is the furnace
and brick-enclosed boiler with
a typical, turban-shaped top,
where the wine is carefully
heated to produce alcohol
vapours.

The alcohol vapours pass
through the swan's-neck pipe,
through the wine warming
chamber, centre, on their
way to the condenser.

The condenser, left, consists
of a spiral pipe immersed
in cold water, where the
alcohol vapour condenses
and trickles out into the
barrel as *eau-de-vie*, ready
for ageing and blending to
create cognac.

99

Most old stills have been converted from wood or coal to natural gas for greater efficiency, like these at Hauteneuve, the vineyard of Alain de Pracomtal in the Grande Champagne area.

The Hennessy distillery *Le Peu*, south-east of Cognac in the heart of cognac country, uses traditional design for pot stills combined with the most modern equipment.

Following pages: distillers must be on hand throughout the process to control the temperature, the alcohol content, the taste.

101

The 'heart' of *eau-de-vie* for cognac averages 70° G.L. at around 15°C. as it leaves the condensation chamber. Fractions from the 'head' and 'tail' are set aside for further treatment.

Alcohol from the second distillation trickles out through a felt filter into a barrel at almost double the strength of cognac in the bottle, thus requiring careful ageing and blending.

Even at this fiery strength, a master distiller like Charles Yvon at Le Peu must taste and smell to control the quality of the *eau-de-vie* which will age to become cognac.

After each distillation, the still must be cleaned, with steam, to remove all traces of residue which might affect the quality of the next batch of *eau-de-vie*.

Once the still is cleaned, the furnace can be fired up again for the next distillation. The process goes on virtually 24 hours a day from autumn to spring.

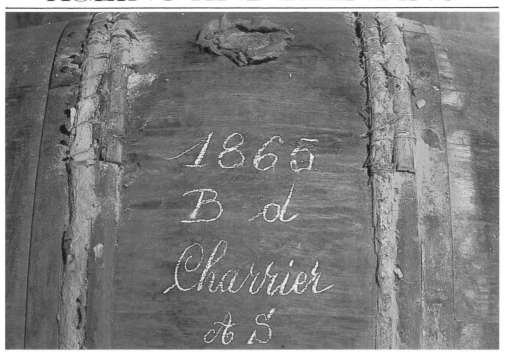

Age is one of the most important characteristics that set cognac apart from other spirits. It is not surprising, therefore, that the long, slow process of creating a rare, old cognac blend which is bottled in the 1980s may have started while Louis XIV was still on the throne, long before Louis XVI and his queen, Marie-Antoinette, lost their heads in the French Revolution.

An acorn fell to the ground somewhere in the cognac region sometime during the reign of Louis XIV. The oak tree that grew from that acorn stood for a hundred years or so before being felled by a forester, perhaps while Napoleon was at the height of his power. The trunk of the felled oak was split into staves which were weathered for at least five years and then fashioned into barrels by a master cooper of Cognac. The barrels were used to store and age *eaux-de-vie de cognac* for a decade or more, perhaps even for a generation, before being filled with cognac distilled about the middle of the 19th century.

Some of that spirit which began ageing in a barrel made from an oak tree growing from an acorn that fell to the ground in cognac country while France's 'Sun King' held glittering court at Versailles may have been blended into the cognac you are sipping from your glass today.

The story of the ageing and blending of cognac must start with the acorn and the oak tree, because cognac takes much of its flavour, aroma and colour from its years spent maturing in oak barrels.

The type of oak from which the barrels are made is important to the ageing of cognac. For a long time Limousin was considered the only suitable wood and it is still preferred by many cognac houses. As the supply of Limousin began to dwindle some coopers turned to Tronçais, and today Tronçais oak is preferred by some cognac houses.

The Limousin is a more classic oak in shape with a broad trunk and widely spreading branches. It grows not in a forest but scattered in meadows, hedgerows and small woods in the area around the city of Limoges to the east of the Charentes. Its wood is wide grained and, when made into barrels, it imparts its tannin to the ageing cognac more slowly than Tronçais.

The Tronçais oak grows thickly in a vast national forest in the centre of France. Because the trees grow close together, they grow very tall, sometimes as high as 90 feet, and the grain of the wood is much closer together. Although the wood contains less tannin, barrels made from Tronçais oak impart their tannin to the cognac more quickly.

The best barrels for ageing cognac, whether Limousin or Tronçais, are made from trees about 100-years old or even older. Only the straight section of the trunk is used. Rough staves are split from the timber rather than sawn so as not to disturb the grain. The staves are then stacked in the open with plenty of air space and left to weather for four or five years in the sun, wind and rain. When the weathered staves reach the cooperage, they are carefully planed down to the correct size and shape for barrel making.

The cooper's craft is an ancient and fascinating one and has changed little over the centuries; almost all of the work of fashioning barrels is still being done by hand. For anyone interested in learning more about coopering there is no better place than Cognac.

One can start at Hennessy who have created a large and impressive museum of cooperage, almost certainly the most complete in the world. The Hennessy museum (which also includes a smaller section on wine making and cognac distilling) is open to the public and contains scores of coopers' tools and other artifacts, many of which are more than a century old. There is also a large tableau recreating a 19th-century cooperage. Most of the museum pieces come from the collection of Jean Taransaud, Master Cooper of Cognac, who has written and published an illustrated book on the cooper's craft, *Le Livre de la Tonnellerie* (unfortunately only available in French).

A number of cognac houses maintain their own cooperages for making and repairing or just repairing barrels. There are also many independent cooperages in the cognac region, the largest being Jean Taransaud's which has been in his family for more than two centuries and which is now owned by Hennessy.

How the barrels are used in ageing cognac is even more important than how they are made. Just as *eau-de-vie de cognac* changes its character by contact with the wood of the barrel, so the wood of the barrel changes character by contact with the spirit. The cognac and the barrel start ageing together, they mature together and they grow old together. Cognac firms have as much respect for a very old barrel as they have for a very old cognac; the one cannot do without the other.

There are several complex interactions between the cognac and the barrel, the most important being the release of tannin from the oak and the slow oxidation and evaporation of the cognac through the pores of the wood.

Newly distilled *eau-de-vie* should, ideally, be left in new barrels only for the first year.

The year-old cognac is then transferred to two- or three-year-old barrels and left for two years.

After seven years in contact with the cognac, a barrel is referred to as a '*barrique rousse*' and is ready for use in ageing the older cognacs.

It is only after 10 or 12 years, however, that a barrel is considered old enough to be used for ageing the more delicate, *distingués* cognacs, such as 15-year-old Grande Champagne. By then the oak has lost virtually all its tannin and thus imparts little to the cognac; oxidation continues albeit more slowly.

But even after 12 years, a barrel continues to age, as does the cognac. With occasional repairs a barrel can be used for 20, 40, 50 years or more. The most precious old cognacs in Hennessy's *le Chai du Fondateur*, for example, reach their peak of maturity in barrels at least half a century old. Such venerable wood has given up all its tannin and oxidation through its pores is very slow indeed.

Cognac cannot remain in the barrel for all of its life. At a certain age, depending on how it has matured, the cognac must be removed because too long a relationship with the oak would add nothing to its character and might even be harmful. Cognacs more than 100 years old are usually taken out of the barrels and stored in demi-johns to await blending. Unlike wine, cognac does not change when sealed in glass.

There are well over two million barrels of cognac ageing in the cognac region in any one year. The largest stocks are held by Hennessy and Martell; Hennessy alone usually have around 180,000 barrels in their warehouses at any one time.

It is the *maître de chais* of a cognac house who presides over the ageing, just as he has carefully controlled the growing of grapes and the making and distilling of the wine. A *maître de chais* must use great expertise in selecting *eaux-de-vie* for ageing. As the larger cognac firms produce only a small percentage of the *eaux-de-vie* they need for blending, most of it comes from independent suppliers. Some firms rely on middlemen, or brokers, to supply them with cognac. Others prefer to deal directly with independent producers whom they know and trust. Hennessy's *maître de chais*, Maurice Fillioux, deals with some 2,500 individual wine growers and distillers, most of whom have supplied Hennessy for decades, if not generations. These independent producers are in constant consultation with Hennessy about methods of viniculture, viticulture and distillation. The shelves, tables and desks in Maurice Fillioux's large office are usually covered with small sample bottles of *eaux-de-vie*, new and old, and he and his assistants are in almost daily contact with various suppliers.

When the cognacs of various vintages and from different growth districts of the region have aged to the satisfaction of the *maître de chais*, he must decide how to blend them in the style of the several types and qualities his firm bottles and sells.

Most of the better-known cognac exporting houses produce about five basic blends and only very rarely change their styles. At Hennessy, for example, there have been only four 'new' blends this century. Names, labels, bottles and packaging change more frequently to conform with marketing fashions.

A *maître de chais* may work for several years to perfect a new style of cognac. Once it has been established, he is faced with the daunting task of maintaining its consistency to the satisfaction of the consumer year after year.

Blending is a most daunting task because of the many thousands of choices the *maître de chais* has between cognacs from different vineyards in different growth areas any of which have been aged for several years or several generations. Time after time he must choose those which will marry to match the taste and quality of a master blend.

Some styles and qualities of cognacs are less complex, so less difficult to blend than others. But the blend for a very fine, rare old cognac at or near the top of the range of a reputable firm may include as many as 20 different cognacs from a dozen vineyards and distilleries in the best three or four growth areas. Some of those selected may have aged since, for example, the 1950s; others, since the 1880s, and others during the intervening decades.

Obviously there could not be nearly enough cognac from the same vineyards and vintages to repeat exactly the same blend to satisfy consumer demand for millions of bottles over the years or, in some cases, millions of bottles in a single year. So the blends change time after time, although the taste and quality of style should not.

A V.S. or V.S.O.P. from Martell or Hennessy, for example, should taste the same in the glass regardless of when the bottle is purchased, following the style of the house.

Blending goes on throughout the year and is all part of a day's work for a *maître de chais*, so much so that even Maurice Fillioux was surprised when we made a rough calculation and discovered that, on average, he produces another blend every single working day of his life.

Monsieur Fillioux, who represents the sixth generation of the Fillioux family to provide *maîtres de chais* to Hennessy, firmly believes that a *maître de chais* must have a gift, inherited or not. He compares the gift for ageing and blending cognac with the gift for music a musician must have to become a successful composer and conductor. Like the musician, the *maître de chais* must develop his gift through years of training and experience, experience above all. He must develop an unerring memory for taste and aroma which enables him to judge without hesitation the most subtle nuances of quality and style of various cognacs, whether freshly distilled or aged for a century or more.

According to Maurice Fillioux, the art of blending cognac is no less complex than that of composing a symphony and then conducting that symphony in the same style, performance after performance, to give pleasure to very demanding and discerning audiences around the world.

114

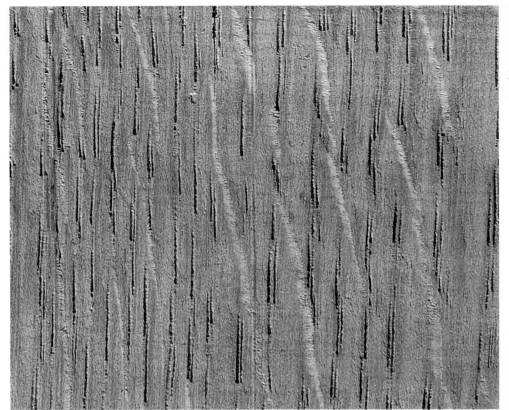

The barrels for ageing cognac are traditionally made from only two types of oak, grown in France. Some cognac houses prefer barrels of Limousin oak, others are partial to Tronçais oak, but both are suitable for ageing cognac.

The Limousin oak, with its spreading branches, grows in meadows and hedgerows around the town of Limoges, to the east of Cognac. Barrel staves show an open grain.

The Tronçais oak grows tall in a national forest in the centre of France, more distant from Cognac. The grain of this oak is closer than that of Limousin.

The craft of coopering (barrel-making) has changed little over the centuries. The adze, a basic tool of the cooper, hardly differs from those used hundreds of years ago. Its owner, working in a modern cooperage outside Cognac, uses an old wagon wheel hub to keep his axe.

There is a cooperage museum at Hennessy in Cognac which preserves historic items: the hand-made seal of a master cooper, 18th century; a small cognac cask carried by Napoleon's troopers; a cooper's plane decorated with ivory, all from the Taransaud collection.

Because every barrel must be made by hand, no two are exactly the same. The cooper chooses just the right staves to fit his barrel and assembles them with great care.
The oak staves are slowly bent into shape, using heat from a fire of oak chips, while the staves are kept damp and drawn together by steel cables from a winch and hoops of iron.

Once the barrel has been shaped, galvanized hoops replace those of iron and the outside of the barrel is planed and sanded. The top and bottom of the barrel are put together by joining pieces of oak cut to size. Only wooden pegs and split reeds are used in the assembly.

Following pages: the oak barrels and vats made by the coopers of Cognac, like these in the warehouse of Delamain in Jarnac, should last for a generation or more. The older the barrel the more valuable it is for ageing cognac.

Preparing for the annual inventory of ageing stocks, Hennessy warehouse workers draw samples from the barrels and mark them with chalk, ready for tasting by the *maître de chais* and his assistants.

Following pages: Tasting takes place in Hennessy's hallowed *le Chai du Fondateur*.

After the alcohol content of each sample is measured *maître de chais* Maurice Fillioux and his assistants taste, pass judgement and record how each batch of ageing cognac has changed from the previous year.

The Fillioux family has provided seven generations of tasters for Hennessy. In Maurice Fillioux's office, his nephew Yann assists him and will be his successor. On the wall is a portrait of Maurice's father and a bas-relief plaque portraying his grandfather, who were in their times *maîtres de chais*.

The tasting and blending rooms of cognac houses are kept immaculately clean. Glasses are washed in clear water only. Blue glasses are sometimes used for tasting so that the colour of the cognac does not influence the taster's judgement.

The *maître de chais* tastes thousands of samples from his suppliers each year, both new *eaux-de-vie* and aged cognac.

As many as 19 or 20 different cognacs of varying ages and from different growth areas may go into the blend for cognacs of the highest quality.

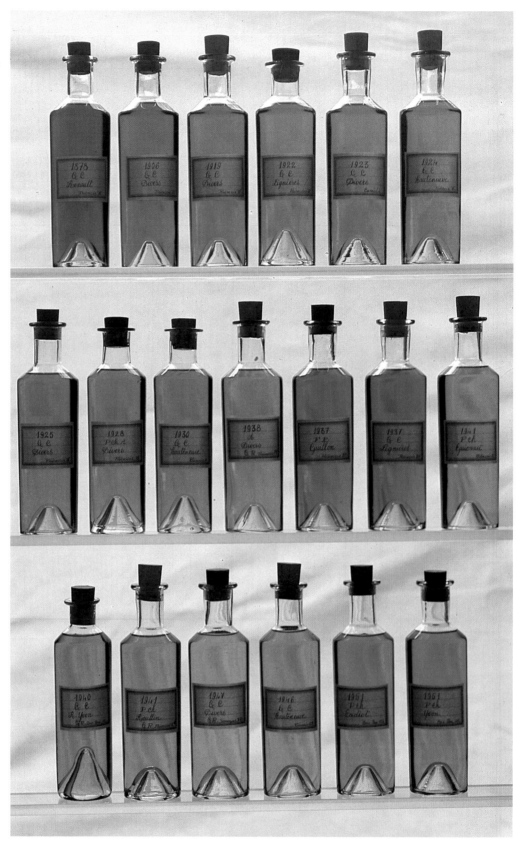

Once the taster has selected cognacs for a blend, they are carefully measured out to make a small sample in proportion. After a final tasting of the sample to check his judgement, the *maître de chais* gives orders for the blend to be made up in quantity.

Following pages: The blending prior to bottling takes place in vast tanks or wooden vats like these at Martell.

THE PLEASURE

Once upon a time everyone's idea of the classic cognac drinker was a ruddy-faced Englishman of substantial build and advanced years smoking a large Havana cigar and sipping expensive cognac from an over-sized balloon glass after dinner in his London club. One tended to think of characters from P.G. Wodehouse and Somerset Maugham or real-life characters such as Churchill, whom the more traditional writers on wines and spirits delight in quoting when discussing cognac.

Certainly it is true that an elegant private dinner or a public banquet anywhere in the world would not be complete without a fine, old cognac served with the coffee.

But to imply that cognac is or ever has been a drink exclusive to the very wealthy or to a particular social class is not only misleading but also historically inaccurate. Even in the early 18th century, when it first began to build its reputation around the world, cognac was considered by all levels of society a strong spirit of superior quality. Up until the First World War when the working man of England, for example, wanted strong drink, his choice was largely between rot-gut gin and cognac, and he was often willing to spend more to enjoy, and to be seen enjoying, the superior product. After scotch whisky began to gain acceptance, cognac still held its own as the more prestigious spirit in working men's clubs and pubs as well as in private clubs frequented by members of the establishment.

There are more true to life images than those of elderly gentlemen in London clubs, who only represent an infinitesimal part of the many millions of cognac drinkers around the world. One thinks instead of the French farmer at the zinc bar of his local café, cradling a very small, balloon-shaped glass in his hands to warm and bring out the aroma of the cognac; the Chinese businessman at a restaurant in Hong Kong with a full bottle of superior cognac on the table, to be consumed with water and ice during an excellent meal much as one might drink a fine wine; the English coalminer in his Newcastle club following his beer with a cognac chaser; the rich matron in Miami pouring liqueur cognac into crystal glasses to accompany the coffee after her charity luncheon.

It is therefore impossible to draw an accurate profile of a 'typical' cognac drinker. Cognac, more than any other spirit, appears to have been accepted as a common denominator of quality among drinkers of the world regardless of nationality, sex, social position or financial status, even though it is, and must remain, an expensive spirit because of the costly way it must be produced.

A brief visit to any wine and spirits outlet will provide an easy cost comparison, although price differentials may vary from country to country. At the lower end of the ranges a bottle of Three-Star or V.S. cognac is likely to cost a quarter to a third more than a proprietary brand of scotch, bourbon, gin, vodka or an ordinary grape brandy. There is a similar or greater price differential between, say, a V.S.O.P. cognac on the one hand and a 'luxury' blended or single malt scotch on the other (gin, vodka, rum and others being left far behind). At the top end of the scale, rare old cognacs may be 50–100% more costly than the most expensive of all other spirits. Put this old cognac into an elaborate crystal decanter and the price rises yet again, although needless to say the quality of the cognac is not improved by the price of the container.

Despite the high cost of cognac compared with other, lesser spirits, and despite a world-wide recession as we entered the 1980s, the demand for cognac has been maintained and even increased in certain parts of the world.

It was England which, more than 300 years ago, provided the initial impetus to an international trade in the excellent *eau-de-vie* of the Charente area of France, and the British Isles have remained over the centuries one of cognac's most loyal customers. By the last two decades of the 20th century, however, the geographical distribution of cognac had become nothing short of phenomenal. Of around 130,000,000 bottles of cognac being sold each year in the 1980s, there was a marked similarity in total consumption between the most important market groups: United Kingdom and Ireland; North America; the Far East; continental Europe, and the domestic French market.

Naturally patterns of distribution and consumption vary from year to year. Hong Kong, for example, not ony increased imports by 28% in one year, securing its place as the country with the greatest per capita consumption, but took 80% of its congac in the superior qualities. In the same year Japan increased its consumption by 17%, and Switzerland increased its imports by a record 41%. In the United States cognac must compete with some very good California grape brandies, but despite this America became the number one export market for cognac as we entered the 1980s. Cognac production and export figures for any one year are available from the trade's governing body, the Bureau National Interprofessionnel du Cognac.

We have explained earlier that the Bureau's control over all aspects of cognac extends to labelling. Correct labelling is important to the consumer not only because it guarantees the authenticity of cognac, but also because it indicates in a general way the age of the cognac.

It is illegal to include on a cognac label, or in advertising, a precise indication of age, such as '5 Years Old', '15 Years Old', or '50 Years Old'. Instead the cognac bureau authorises certain categories of names which may be used to designate the minimum ages in any blend. The name 'Three Star' or 'V.S.', for example, indicates a blend containing no cognac less than three-years old, and such blends will certainly include older cognacs as well. A 'V.S.O.P.' or 'Reserve' blend from a reputable house will always be substantially older, although the legal minimum is only four years. The top category, which includes very old cognacs, allows the use of names like 'Cordon Noir', 'Napoléon', 'Extra', 'Paradis'. The legal minimum is however a modest six years. Clearly, therefore, these official name categories do not always do full justice to the true age of cognac. Whilst a V.S.O.P. blend may include cognacs as young as four years, it may also contain some twenty years old. In the best blends of the top category one may well find cognacs more than 100 years old. The rules, nevertheless, remain categorical; no firm may boast of the average age of a blend, however venerable.

Regardless of whether you prefer your cognac as a long drink before lunch, Chinese-style with a meal, or as an after-dinner digestive, the best way to make an initial choice is to taste cognac on its own.

The type of glass you choose will depend on how you drink your cognac, but for a serious, first tasting you would do best to follow the example of the Charentais who created cognac and who, be they simple wine farmers or scions of the great cognac firms, almost invariably savour it on its own. There are three types of glasses used in the cognac region: one is tulip shaped; another is similar in shape to the typical sherry *copita;* and the third is balloon shaped but of moderate size (the over-sized balloon glass is considered more suitable for goldfish than cognac). These shapes were conceived to fit into the palm of the hand which gently warms the cognac, releasing its aromas which are concentrated towards the nose by the shape of the glass. The glass should be thin enough and the quantity of cognac poured into it modest enough so that the warmth of the hand is sufficient. No true lover of cognac would allow the smell of an alcohol burner in the same room, much less use such an apparatus to heat the glass.

The first impression, as you raise your glass to your lips and nose, is the aroma; then as you sip the cognac comes the taste, ideally a warm but not harsh sensation. You may or may not detect, through your different senses, a certain fullness, a roundness from the fruit with out the actual taste of grape; a slightly woody taste from the oak of the barrels; a mellowness that comes from age; and above all an authority and character unlike those found in any other spirit. The character of the cognac created by each house will be different; the choice is yours . . . .

Any discussion of the pleasures of cognac would be incomplete without a passing reference to other means of enjoyment, apart from pouring it directly from the bottle to the glass. Few of us need to be reminded of the gastronomic delights of cooking with cognac, and any good cookbook will include recipes for sauces, marinades, flambés, soufflés and other dishes using cognac to impart a special flavour and elegance. Most chefs recommend that you use a cognac of V.S.O.P. quality. Given the small amounts required, it is a false economy to use an ordinary cognac – and certainly not a 'cooking brandy' – if you are striving for *haute cuisine*. A superior cognac also contributes to the morale of the cook, who might take a sip or two while stirring the sauce.

There are numerous delicacies made from fresh fruits or chestnuts preserved in cognac, as well as sweet liqueurs with a cognac base. Many of the cognac-based liqueurs have a limited, domestic reputation, but some are known internationally, notably Grand Marnier with its distinctive orange and cognac flavour and 'B and B', the blend of Benedictine and a cognac of strength and character.

The most original by-product of cognac is, without doubt, *pineau des Charentes,* original in that for many years before it achieved any commercial success, it was made and drunk by the wine farmers and distillers of the cognac region and so is a truly regional drink. Pineau is, quite simply, a marriage of must, fresh from the grape press, with cognac; roughly three parts of must to one of cognac. The alcohol of the cognac inhibits the fermentation of the grape must which would otherwise become wine. The result, after ageing, is a pleasant apéritif best served cold, which combines the sweet flavour of the grape with the authority of the cognac.

Pineau, like cognac, may be bought by the roadside in the cognac region or direct from small distillers. By all means try some of the locally distributed cognac if you are in the area.

Many excellent products are available, although their quality is not always as consistent over a period of time as that of the larger firms, whose considerable stocks enable blending to a regular pattern.

But there are no rules about cognac drinking; the only criteria are, and should be, your taste and pleasure.

Bottles for Rémy-Martin coming off the production line at the giant glassworks in Cognac which supplies most of the cognac houses.

Some cognac houses, large and small, still label special stocks by hand, as workers are doing here at Delamain in Jarnac.

The larger cognac houses selling millions of bottles a year around the world maintain the most modern bottling plants, like that of Hennessy shown here.

Preceding pages: 'Louis' serves a fine, old cognac after a late lunch at Logis de Dion, a former royal hunting lodge now owned by Alain de Pracomtal, President of Hennessy.

These four types of glasses, shown to scale, are those preferred in cognac country. The over-inflated balloon glass is rarely used in the region.

Some cognac houses make use of their large distilling halls for promotions and local events, like this lunch for a wine club at Hennessy's Le Peu and the annual workers' party in Bisquit's distillery.

Although cognac is a versatile spirit for mixed drinks, it is best appreciated on its own to revive one's spirits after a hard day's work in the vineyards or with coffee after a business lunch.

Following pages: Leaders of the cognac houses and representatives of the vineyard owners meet regularly to agree regional policy. All are members of the Bureau National Interprofessionnel du Cognac, governing body of the trade which controls quality by very strict regulations.

A retired cognac worker makes *pineau* from grapes from his own, small vineyard: three parts of fresh grape juice to one part of cognac is the recipe for this popular local apéritif which is now being exported.

APPENDICES

There are more than 200 firms officially registered as *négociants*, merchants who age, blend and sell cognac. The list varies from year to year; a complete and current list for each year is available from the Bureau National Interprofessionnel du Cognac, 3 Allées de la Corderie, 16101 Cognac (telephone 826670). In our appendix Some of the Cognac Houses, we present information about those firms most likely to be known to our readers, based on details supplied by the firms themselves.

Cognac is best appreciated on its own, but it is also the most versatile of spirits as an ingredient in mixed drinks: the list of cognac cocktails is endless. We asked Louis Bertin, retired as Hennessy's major-domo after some 50 years service with the family and firm, to list some of his favourites for our appendix Mixing with Cognac. (His 'measure' is 1½ fluid ounces, his 'dash' about six drops.)

The many excellent books on French cuisine contain numerous recipes with cognac as a vital ingredient. For our appendix Cooking with Cognac, we asked Chef Cuisinier Michel Dupont of Hennessy to give a few of his own recipes for the gourmet meals served to important guests of Hennessy in Cognac. Before dealing with haute cuisine, however, Chef Dupont describes two simple dishes typical of the Charente region.

Although many of the terms most frequently used in the creation of cognac have already been explained in text or captions, we include as an appendix a Glossary as a ready guide to the terminology, giving the term in French and the definition in English.

Our basic map shows vineyard areas, some towns, roads and locations we photographed. For a general tour of the region, see Michelin's scale 1:200,000 maps Nos. 71 and 72. For a closer look at the heartland of cognac country, use scale 1:25,000 maps from the *Institut Geographique National*, Nos. 16/32 *Ouest* and 16/32 *Est*.

AUGIER Frères & Co.
Established 1643 (oldest of existing cognac
    houses).
Place de la Salle Verte, B.P. 48, 16100 Cognac.
Telephone 45–820001.
Visits by clients only for tours of *chais* and
    tasting.
Range of cognacs includes Three Star,
    V.S.O.P. Napoléon.

BISQUIT, Department of Ricard S.A.
Established 1819.
Domaine de Lignères, B.P. 15, 16170
    Rouillac.
Telephone 45–965511.
All visitors welcome in summer, otherwise by
    appointment, for tours of *chais* and
    other facilities with tasting and
    souvenirs.
Range of cognacs includes Three Star,
    V.S.O.P., Napoléon, Extra Vieille Or.

CAMUS "La Grande Marque" S.A.
Established 1863.
29 Rue Marguerite de Navarre, B.P. 19,
    16101 Cognac CEDEX.
Telephone 45–322828.
All visitors welcome in summer, otherwise by
    appointment, for tours of *chais* and
    vineyards with tasting and souvenirs.
Range of cognacs includes Celebration, Grand
    V.S.O.P., Napoléon, X.O.

CASTILLON RENAULT S.A.
Established 1814.
23 Rue du Port, B.P. 7, 16101 Cognac
    CEDEX.
Telephone 45–825288.
Visits by clients only.
Range of cognacs includes V.S., V.S.O.P.,
    Carte Noire Extra, X.O., O.V.B. Old
    Vintage Blend.

COURVOISIER S.A.
Established 1835.
Place du Château, B.P. 59, 16200 Jarnac.
Telephone 45–810411.
All visitors welcome for tours of *chais* and
    other facilities with audio-visuals,
    museum, shop.
Range of cognacs includes Three Star Luxe,
    V.S.O.P., Napoléon, Extra Vieille.

DELAMAIN & Co.
Established 1824.
5–7 Rue Jacques et Robert Delamain, B.P. 16,
    16200 Jarnac.
Telephone 45–810824.
Visitors by appointment only for tours of *chais*
    and tasting.
Range of cognacs includes Grande
    Champagne Pale and Dry, Fine
    Champagne Vesper, Très Vieux Grand
    Champagne.

HARDY, A, & Co.
Established 1863.
142 Rue Basse de Crouin, B.P. 27, 16 100
    Cognac.
Telephone 45–825955.
Visits by appointment only.
Range of cognacs includes Three Star, Fine
    Champagne V.S.O.P., Fine Champagne
    Napoléon, Noces D'Argent, Grande
    Champagne Noces D'Or.

HENNESSY, Société JA[S], & Co.
Established 1765.
1 Rue de la Richonne, B.P. 20, 16101 Cognac
    CEDEX.
Telephone 45–825222.
All visitors welcome for tours of *chais* and
    other facilities, large museum of cognac
    and cooperage with audio-visuals,
    souvenirs, shop (group visits can be
    arranged).
Range of cognacs includes V.S., V.S.O.P. Fine
    Champagne, Napoléon, X.O., Paradis.

HINE, Cognac, S.A.
Established 1763.
16 Quai de l'Orangerie, 16200 Jarnac.
Telephone 45−811138.
Visitors by appointment only for tours of *chais*
    with audio-visuals, souvenirs.
Range of cognacs includes Three Star,
    V.S.O.P., Antique, Old Vintage.

LARSEN, Societe, S.A.
Established 1926.
54 Boulevard de Paris, B.P. 41, 16102 Cognac
    CEDEX.
Telephone 45−820588.
All visitors welcome for tours of *chais* with
    tasting, souvenirs.
Range of cognacs includes Special, T.V.F.C.,
    Napoleon, Drakkar Invincible.

MARTELL & Co.
Established 1715.
Place E. Martell, B.P. 21, 16101 Cognac
    CEDEX.
Telephone 45-824444.
All visitors welcome for tours of *chais* and
    other facilities, with audio-visuals,
    tasting, souvenirs.
Range of cognacs includes V.S. Three Star,
    Médallion V.S.O.P., Cordon Noir,
    Cordon Bleu, Cordon Argent Extra.

MONNET, J.G., & Co.
Established 1838.
52 Avenue Paul Firino Martell, B.P. 22, 16100
    Cognac CEDEX.
Telephone 45−825711.
Visits by clients only by appointment.
Range of cognacs includes Three Star
    Tradition, V.S.O.P., Napoléon, X.O.

OTARD, Cognac, S.A.
Established 1795.
Château de Cognac, B.P. 3, 16101 Cognac
    CEDEX.
Telephone 45−824000.
All visitors welcome for tours of *chais* and
    other facilities, *son et lumière* in
    château, tasting, shop.
Range of cognacs includes Three Star/V.S.,
    V.S.O.P. Fine Champagne Baron Otard,
    Napoléon, Princes de Cognac, X.O.

POLIGNAC, Prince Hubert de.
Established 1929.
49 Rue Lohmeyer, B.P. 35, 16102 Cognac
    CEDEX.
Telephone 45−824577.
Visitors welcome spring and summer for tours
    of *chais* and other facilities with audio-
    visuals and tasting.
Range of cognacs includes Three Star,
    V.S.O.P. Fine Champagne, Napoléon
    Fine Champagne, Dynasty Grande Fine
    Champagne.

REMY-MARTIN & Co.
Established 1724
20 Rue de la Société Vinicole, B.P. 37, 16102
    Cognac CEDEX.
Telephone 45−824111.
Visitors by appointment only for tours of *chais*
    with tasting.
Range of cognacs includes Three Star,
    V.S.O.P. Fine Champagne, Centaure
    Napoléon, X.O., Louis XIII Grande
    Champagne.

SALIGNAC, L. de, & Cie.
Established 1809.
Domaine du Breuil, Rue Robert Daugas, B.P.
    4, 16100 Cognac CEDEX.
Telephone 45−810411.
Visits by clients only by appointment.
Range of cognacs includes Three Star,
    V.S.O.P., Très Vieille Fine Cognac
    Napoléon.

COGNAC A L'ORANGE Pour 1 measure of cognac into a glass, add 3–5 measures of fresh orange juice, some ice and a half-slice of orange as decoration. Refreshing at any time of the day, a classic favourite in cognac country.

PRINCE OF WALES Put some ice in a stemmed glass, pour in 1 measure of cognac, 1½ measures dry champagne, 2 dashes Angostura and 2 dashes Curacao. Stir.

COGNAC FIZZ Pour 1½ measures of cognac into a glass, add 1 tsp. sugar, juice of ½ lemon and ½ lime, ice and sparkling water. Stir.

SIDE-CAR Shake with ice 2 measures cognac, 1 measure Cointreau, 1 measure lemon juice. Strain into a glass.

STINGER Mix with cracked ice 1 measure cognac, 1 measure creme de menthe. Pour into a tall glass, with the ice.

ALEXANDRA Shake with cracked ice 1 measure cognac, 1 measure creme de cacao, 1 measure fresh cream. Strain into a glass.

HORSE'S NECK Pour into a glass 1½ measures cognac, 2 dashes Angostura, add ice and dry ginger ale.

COGNAC FANCY Stir with ice 1 measure cognac, 1 dash orange bitters, 1 dash Angostura, then strain into a cocktail glass.

EGG FIZZ Shake with ice cubes 1 measure cognac, 1 oz. lemon juice, 1 raw egg, 1 tsp. granulated sugar. Strain into glass, add soda water to taste.

PORTO FLIP Shake with ice cubes ½ measure cognac, 1 measure port, 1 raw egg. Strain into a cocktail glass and add grated nutmeg.

COOKING WITH COGNAC

HUITRES ET SAUCISSES A LA CHARENTAISE
Oysters and sausages Charente style

Bring to table a large platter of raw oysters on the half-shell, allowing at least six per person; a large dish of finger-sized, very spicy sausages, served hot; French bread, unsalted butter and lemon wedges. Each person serves himself.

MELON AU PINEAU DES CHARENTES
Melon flavoured with pineau.

Allow half a melon per person. Cut melons in half and remove seeds and pulp. Scoop out the flesh with a melon scoop or a round spoon to make small balls. Reserve the melon shells. Pour a generous amount of white pineau over the balls and leave to marinate in the refrigerator for an hour or so. Fill melon shells with the balls, pour over remaining pineau-flavoured juice and serve.

SOUFFLE DE FOIE DE VOLAILLES AU COGNAC
Chicken liver pâté garnished with cognac-flavoured aspic.

750 gr. (1½ lb.) chicken livers
300 gr. (10 fl. oz.) crème fraîche
4 eggs, separated
50 gr. (2 oz.) sugar
15 gr. (1½ oz.) salt
pepper and allspice

Purée the chicken livers in a blender, then pass through a sieve. Beat the crème fraîche with the egg yolks, season with sugar, salt, a pinch each of pepper and allspice and add to the chicken livers. Fold in stiffly beaten egg whites and pour mixture into a terrine. Place the terrine in a baking dish containing boiling water and cook in a moderate oven for 25–30 minutes. When cold, slice the pâté and serve each slice on toast with a garnish of cognac-flavoured aspic, with slices of tomato and a lettuce leaf.

BRIOCHE DE RIS DE VEAU AUX LANGOUSTINES

Brioches filled with sweetbreads in cognac sauce and crayfish. For 4 persons.

12 crayfish
500 gr. (1 lb. 1 oz.) sweetbreads
300 gr. (10 fl. oz.) double cream
1/2 lt. (17 fl. oz.) veal stock
60 gr. (2 oz.) unsalted butter
8 cl. (3 fl. oz.) VSOP cognac
4 medium-sized brioches

Cook the crayfish in slightly salted water until just pink. Separate the heads from the tails and remove the shells from the tails. Cook the heads in the stock for about 10 minutes, then strain, discarding heads. Braise the prepared sweetbreads in half the stock, remove from the pan and strain the stock again. Add the rest of the stock, reduce by half, then add the cream and cognac, stirring until well blended. Add butter and season. Add sweetbreads, thickly sliced, and keep hot in sauce. While warming the brioches in the oven, fry the crayfish tails over a high heat for about 1 minute. Fill brioches with the sweetbreads in their sauce, arrange crayfish tails on top and serve.

MAGRETS DE CANARD A LA FINE CHAMPAGNE ET POIVRE VERT

Breast of duck in a sauce of cognac and green peppercorns. For 4–5 persons.

2 large fillets of duck breast with the skin left on
1/2 lt. (17 fl. oz.) strongly flavoured stock
300 gr. (10 fl. oz.) double cream
100 gr. (3 1/2 fl. oz.) unsalted butter
1 tbls. green peppercorns
1 glass VSOP Fine Champagne cognac

Season the duck fillets with salt and pepper; turn quickly in a little oil in a frying pan over a high heat until golden brown. Remove the fillets to an oven dish and cook for approx. 10 minutes (oven mark 5–6) until just pink inside. Meanwhile, drain oil from frying pan, leaving the juices, deglaze with the cognac and flambé. Add stock to the pan and reduce by a quarter. Add cream and reduce again, stirring until well-blended. Add butter and green peppercorns and blend into sauce. Remove skin from the fillets, slice into portions, cover with the sauce and serve.

EMINCE DE LAPEREAUX AU RAISINS FRAIS ET COGNAC

Rabbit with grapes and cognac. For 4–5 persons.

1 dressed rabbit, approx. 1.7 kg. (3 3/4 lb.)
2 bunches of Muscat grapes
250 gr. (9 fl. oz.) crème fraîche
50 gr. (1 3/4 oz.) unsalted butter
1 tbls. oil
5 cl. (2 fl. oz.) cognac

Joint the rabbit, remove the meat from the bones and cut into thick slices. Purée the raw liver. Skin the grapes from one bunch and squeeze the juice from the second. Season the rabbit meat with a little salt and pepper and brown quickly in the oil and butter for about 2 minutes. Add the cognac and reduce the liquid by half. Add the grape juice and crème fraîche and check seasoning. If necessary, add a little stock so the meat is three-quarters covered. Simmer for 12–15 minutes until the meat is tender. Add the pureed liver and bring to the boil. Add the peeled grapes and serve.

PANNEQUETS FLAMBES A LA FINE CHAMPAGNE

Crêpes with sweet stuffing, flamed in cognac. For 4 persons.

8 sweet crêpes, already prepared
1/2 lt. (two generous cups) confectioner's custard, already prepared
125 gr. (4 oz.) chopped, candied fruit or chopped marrons glacés
15 cl. (5 fl. oz.) VSOP Fine Champagne cognac

Soften the candied fruit or marrons glacés in a little of the cognac and add to the custard. Coat each crêpe with a generous portion of this mixture. Roll up each crêpe and place them in a buttered, flame-proof dish. Leave in a slow oven until thoroughly hot. Remove from the oven, flambé immediately with the rest of the cognac and serve.

acquit jaune d'or French government document certifying authenticity of cognac.

alambic charentais Copper pot still traditionally used in the Charente region, the only type allowed by law for distillation of cognac.

barrique Oak barrel used for ageing cognac, traditionally with a capacity of 270 litres, now more often 300–350 litres.

Bois Communs or Bois Ordinaires The sixth of officially-designed *crus*, vineyard areas, in the cognac region.

bonne chauffe The second distillation of cognac, as required by law.

Borderies The smallest, but much-favoured of the officially-designated cognac vineyard areas.

bouilleurs de cru Cognac distillers who distil only their own wine.

bouilleurs de profession Distillers of cognac who distil wine from other growers.

brouillis The low-strength alcohol resulting from a first distillation of the wine, which is re-distilled in the *bonne chauffe* to produce cognac.

chapiteau The top of the boiler of a cognac still where alcohol vapours collect before passing to the condenser chamber; variously onion-shaped or turban-shaped.

chaudière The boiler of a cognac still in which wine is heated to produce alcohol vapours.

chauffe-vin A chamber used in most cognac stills to pre-heat the wine before it reaches the boiler.

coeur The 'heart' of alcohol set aside for cognac, left after less desirable fractions are discarded.

col de cygne A 'swan's neck' pipe which takes alcohol vapours from the boiler of a cognac still to the condenser; some stills employ a straight pipe instead.

Colombard One of the varieties of grapes still used in cognac; once popular but now rarely grown.

chai The warehouse where cognac is aged in barrels.

cru Vineyard area, of which there are six in the cognac region delimited by law: Grande Champagne, Petite Champagne, Borderies, Fins Bois, Bons Bois, and Bois Communs or Bois Ordinaires.

eau-de-vie Alcohol usually distilled from fruits, and for cognac only from grapes of the region.

Fine Champagne A cognac blended from *eaux-de-vie* originating in the *crus* of Grande Champagne and Petite Champagne only, with at least 50% from the former.

Fins Bois The fourth of the six designated vineyard areas in the cognac region.

Folle Blanche One of the approved varieties of grapes for making cognac, now rarely used.

foudre A large oak cask of greater capacity than the standard barrel.

fourneau The furnace of a cognac still, which must be fired by direct flame, once from solid fuels (wood or coal), now almost exclusively by gas.

Grande Champagne First of the six officially designated vineyard areas for cognac production.

Limousin The region to the east of Cognac, whose fine oak trees are used for making barrels in which to age cognac.

maître de chais The chief taster and blender of a cognac house, usually also responsible for quality control from the vine to the bottle.

phylloxera The root louse which devastated vineyards in the late 19th century, including those of the cognac region; today all vines are grafted using a root stock which is resistant to the pest.

Pineau des Charentes A strong aperitif from the cognac region, produced by adding one part cognac to three parts fresh grape juice, either white or red.

Petite Champagne The second of the six officially designated vineyard areas in the region.

queue The 'tail' fraction of a distillation of cognac which is set aside for re-distillation.

Saint-Emilion des Charentes Local name for the grape variety Ugni Blanc, most favoured of authorized vines for cognac production, accounting for more than 90% of vines in the region.

serpentin The coiled copper pipe in the condenser of a cognac still.

tanin Tannin from the oak barrels which, during the ageing process, gives flavour and colour to the cognac.

tête The 'head' fraction produced during distilling cognac, set aside for further distillation.

tonneau A large vat made as an oak barrel but in the shape of a truncated cone, with a capacity of 10 to 1000 hectolitres, usually for blending cognac.

tonneliers coopers, barrel-makers.

Torula compniacensis richon A black fungus which thrives on alcohol fumes escaping from barrels of ageing cognac.

Tronçais A forest in the centre of France whose oak trees are used for barrels for ageing cognac.

vendange The annual grape harvest; vintage.

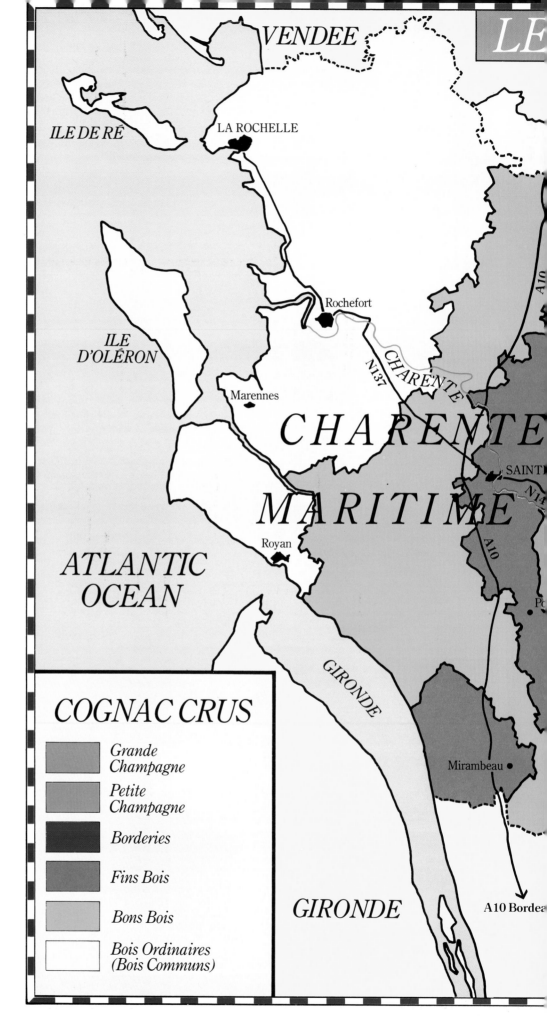

VENDEE

LE

ILE DE RÉ

LA ROCHELLE

Rochefort

CHARENTE

N137

ILE
D'OLÉRON

Marennes

CHARENTE

MARITIME

SAINTE

N14

A10

ATLANTIC
OCEAN

Royan

Po

GIRONDE

Mirambeau •

COGNAC CRUS

Grande
Champagne

Petite
Champagne

Borderies

Fins Bois

Bons Bois

GIRONDE

A10 Bordea

Bois Ordinaires
(Bois Communs)

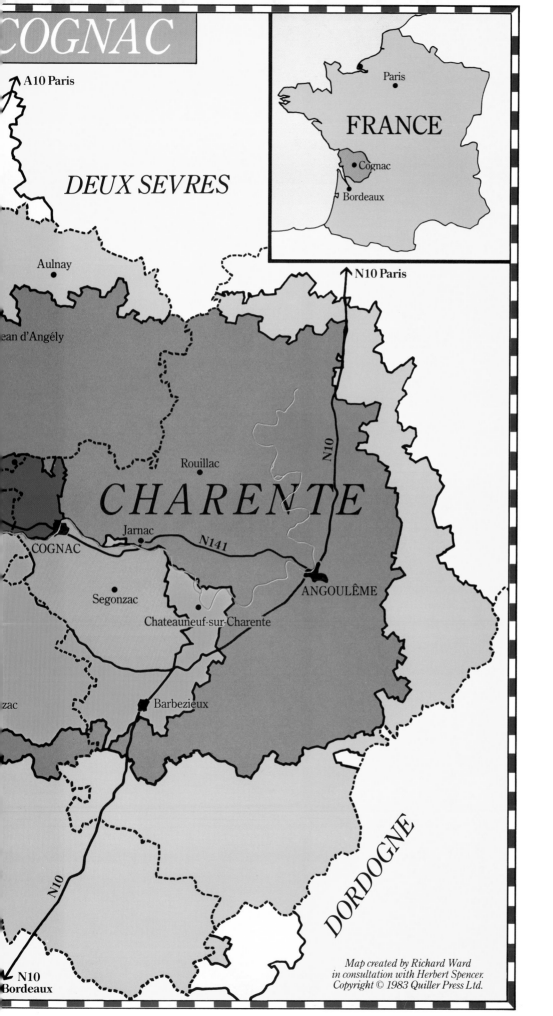

A10 Paris

DEUX SEVRES

Aulnay

ean d'Angély

N10 Paris

FRANCE

Paris

Cognac

Bordeaux

Rouillac

CHARENTE

N10

Jarnac

N141

COGNAC

ANGOULÊME

Segonzac

Chateauneuf-sur-Charente

zac

Barbezieux

DORDOGNE

N10

N10
Bordeaux

159

Map created by Richard Ward
in consultation with Herbert Spencer.
Copyright © 1983 Quiller Press Ltd.